COLORADO INJURY LAW

A Reference for Accident Victims

by Michael R. O'Connell, Esq.

Speaker Media Press

Colorado Injury Law: A Reference for Accident Victims

ISBN 978-1-935411-11-6

Contents

CONTRIBUTING AUTHORS

This book is a collective effort compiled for you by twenty leading members of the plaintiff's bar in the states of Colorado, New York, North Carolina, South Carolina, Texas, Pennsylvania, Arkansas, Florida, Georgia, Indiana, Kentucky, and Tennessee. Each attorney involved has contributed his expertise to this project to assure the reader that they are being provided with basic sound information when they find themselves the victim of an accident. This is not a law book, but an overview of personal injury law.

The O'Connell Law Firm, P.C.
Colorado | www.ColoradoInjuryAttorney.net
Lewis & Daggett, Attorneys at Law, P.A.
North Carolina | www.LewisDaggett.com
Law Offices of Michael A. DeMayo, L.L.P.
North and South Carolina | www.DeMayoLaw.com
Terry Bryant Accident & Injury Law
Texas | www.TerryBryant.com
Rainwater, Holt & Sexton, P.A.
Arkansas | www.CallRainwater.com
Parr Richey Obremskey Frandsen & Patterson
Indiana | www.ParrInjury.com
Martin, Harding & Mazzotti, LLP Attorneys at Law
New York & Vermont | www.1800LAW1010.com
Hagelgans & Veronis
Pennsylvania | www.HVLawfirm.com
Steinger, Iscoe & Greene Injury Lawyers
Florida | www.InjuryLawyers.com
Stokes & Kopitsky P.A.
Georgia | www.StokesInjuryLawyers.com
John Bales Attorneys
Florida | www.JohnBales.com
Hughes & Coleman Injury Lawyers
Kentucky & Tennessee | www.HughesandColeman.com

Additional Editors/Writers:
Sandra K. Rigby
Lorelei Laird

DISCLAIMER

This publication is designed to provide general information regarding personal injury claims and is not intended to be legal advice. It is sold and distributed with the understanding that neither the publisher, nor the authors, nor the contributors, are engaged in rendering legal or other professional services to the reader. If legal advice or other professional assistance is required, the services of a competent professional person should be sought.

The publisher, authors and contributors make no representations or warranties with respect to the accuracy or completeness of the contents of this work and specifically disclaim all warranties, including without limitation warranties of fitness for a particular purpose. No warranty may be created by sales or promotional materials. The advice and strategies contained herein may not be suitable for every situation. Neither the publisher, nor the authors, nor the contributors shall be liable for damages arising herefrom.

As this publication is not intended as legal advice, any use of this information will not create an attorney-client relationship. After an initial consultation, and before representing you on any claim, a written attorney-client agreement must be signed in order to create such a relationship.

FOREWORD

I became involved in this project and wrote this book because I believe in helping people who have been victimized by carelessness. As a U.S. Army veteran, and the son of a police officer, I believe in personal responsibility. I hate the idea of good people being injured by a careless driver, only to be injured again by a faceless insurance company. Throughout my entire legal career I have represented only individuals and families, never a corporation. When an accident caused by someone else's carelessness and negligence threatens your health, your family and your income, you need someone to fight for you. That's what we do.

If you or someone you love has been seriously injured in an accident, you may be wondering what to do next. Who will pay the medical bills? How will you be compensated for lost wages? How does the insurance system work? How does the legal system work? Will you be treated fairly? Is there anyone looking out for your interests? Do you need an attorney? How do you go about finding an attorney you can trust; one who will guide you through the process? What is your claim worth?

Accidents cause serious injuries, pain, emotional trauma, and oftentimes a serious disruption in the lives of everyone involved, including loved ones. To make matters worse, chances are that the accident kept you from working for some period, which took a toll on your income. Maybe you're not sure you'll ever do the same job again. Maybe you're struggling to make ends meet without that income. Maybe the insurance company isn't helping, or you suspect it isn't telling you everything. It's all overwhelming and you know you need help, but you have no idea what to do next.

If that sounds familiar, we wrote this book for you. We want this book to be a guide for people who have been involved in serious accidents, or have family members who were, and have no idea what to do next. After the initial emergency room trip, most people don't know where to turn. And why should they? Thankfully most people don't have a lot of prior experience with serious injuries and the disruption that an accident can cause in the very fabric of life. After an accident, you need to learn a lot of new things about insurance claims, financial obligations, liens, medical conditions and injury law. Even for healthy people, that's a lot to learn all at once. For people who are already struggling with injuries, pain, financial strain and insurance company red tape, it can be overwhelming.

We wrote this book for many reasons. For one thing, we wanted to write a simple, accessible guidebook written without "legalese." Over the years, many of our clients have told us that they wished they had known more about the process earlier. Oftentimes people are intimidated or nervous about the idea of getting involved with insurance claims and lawyers to begin with. We want this book to take some of the mystery, fear, and intimidation out of getting fair and prompt compensation for your claim.

Another important reason we wrote this book is because we want to help protect accident victims from the financial threat posed by insurance companies. Most people assume with good natured trust that insurance companies exist to pay claims and cover the very types of damages that they have sustained. Unfortunately, this is usually not the case. Like all businesses, insurance companies exist to make money. They make money when customers pay premiums. When a party is injured and makes an insurance claim, those same insurance companies lose money. That's especially true with large claims, which is why the most seriously injured people are at the greatest risk of not being compensated fairly. It all boils down to the fact that insurance companies don't want to pay you any more money than they have to. As corporations, they place profits over people.

Over the years we have found that most clients came to us only after getting some type of indication that they were not going to be treated fairly by the insurance company. They didn't start out thinking they needed an attorney, but they are always glad they got one. Perhaps it was an adjuster who was very difficult to reach, or didn't return phone calls. Perhaps it was a representative who was a little too eager to settle a serious claim a little too quickly. Whatever the reason, almost no one regrets the decision to sit down with us and get a better understanding of the process, including the ways to maximize their claim.

We can make a huge difference in the compensation a client will recover, but only if we speak to you before you sign any releases or accept an offer of settlement. We have had to turn away more than one client who learned that lesson too late, and it was painful to do so. If you take nothing else away from this book, we hope you take away the lesson that insurance companies should not be trusted to make things "right". When significant amounts of money are at stake, please consider taking advantage of our free consultations to discuss your situation before signing anything.

Most importantly, we wrote this book to answer your questions. As personal injury attorneys dedicated to helping people protect themselves against corporations with immense resources at their disposal, we came to realize that clients kept coming to us with similar questions. We came to the conclusion that many questions were common to virtually anybody who had been in an accident. This book is an attempt to answer the most common and important questions we get from clients and potential clients.

We know however, that no book can answer every question. Every case is different, and it's only after we hear about your case that we can give you the answers that fit your personal situation. No book can build the same relationship that a face-to-face meeting can. That's why we encourage you to contact us for more information, or if you have questions, suggestions, or concerns. Meeting with potential clients to hear more about their cases is what we do best, and the initial consultation is free!

You can reach us at (303) 759-4000, or find us online at www.ColoradoInjuryAttorney.net. We're here to help.

Michael O'Connell, Esq.

INTRODUCTION

At The O'Connell Law Firm, we are dedicated to helping injured people receive fair, prompt and just compensation. The sad fact is that insurance companies dedicate their enormous resources to paying as little as possible to people who are injured. Our firm only handles cases on behalf of people seeking compensation from the individuals and institutions responsible for their accidents. We are proud to say we've helped hundreds of clients recover the money they need to pay their medical bills, support their families and be fully compensated.

If you've been hurt, you deserve full compensation for what you have lost. Personal injury attorney Michael O'Connell and our office staff help victims of all types of accidents, by providing guidance and skilled representation that can make a big difference in the way your claim is handled and resolved.

We have extensive experience and expertise in handling car accidents, truck accidents, motorcycle crashes, car-pedestrian collisions and premises accidents. At the O'Connell Law Firm, we represent people who have had catastrophic injuries, as well as clients who are just looking to be treated fairly and with dignity.

Colorado's Accident Experts

"From the moment we sat down, they took care of us. Everything from our property damage, to finding a doctor, to answering every question we had. At the end of the day, they got us a settlement that was larger than we ever expected." Ed and Terry C., Denver, CO

We started this firm with the idea of focusing on three things that people told us they want. It's really not complicated. The first thing people want is to have their questions answered, and they want to know what is going to happen next. Secondly, people want their lawyer to take care of all the details so they don't have to worry about anything other than getting back on their feet, physically and financially. Finally, and most importantly, our clients want to get the most money possible to compensate them for what they have been through. We don't worry about being on television or having big fancy offices. We just worry about making sure you get the best settlement possible, the best treatment possible, and peace of mind.

The members of our team, based in Denver, Colorado, have over 50 years of combined experience in law, medicine and complex negotiations. We take the time required to carefully counsel clients injured in accidents on Colorado roadways. We navigate you through the insurance maze and strive to lead you towards personal and financial recovery. We focus on maximizing the value of your claim. This means ascertaining the true extent of your injuries - both financial and personal.

You will almost certainly require significant medical treatment after suffering a serious accident. Delays in obtaining insurance coverage or a financial settlement may hinder your ability to pay for your medical care when you need it. Our firm has a network of medical professionals who will work on a lien basis. They will treat you with the understanding that you currently cannot pay for treatment.

Another key factor in resolving personal injury disputes is the ability to successfully negotiate with insurance providers. Our legal team has extensive experience both litigating and negotiating disputes. Attorney Michael O'Connell has legal and business experience as a negotiator in a variety of complex business and insurance scenarios. We will make sure the insurance company fully understands your situation and determination following a car wreck.

At the O'Connell Law Firm, we have also developed strategic alliances with other law firms and attorneys around the State of Colorado, and around the country. This enables us to bring many different types of resources to a case when required, and enables us to keep costs down. When we keep costs low, the client benefits because of higher "walk-away" settlements and verdicts.

Our staff is smart, dedicated, and absolutely committed to

making the process as smooth as possible for our clients. Our team of paralegals, registered nurses and legal assistants is top notch. We also have a network of top doctors and specialists who are committed to helping people who have been injured in accidents. Often, we can even arrange for someone to be seen by a doctor the same day that they come in to see an attorney for the first time. Our experts can be especially helpful for clients who don't have a regular doctor, don't have insurance or don't like the insurance they have. Our doctors are reasonable, and can be paid out of the settlement. There is no reason to not get the care you need when you need it.

We Have the Experience and Expertise: Don't be Hurt Twice

"We were lost. There was so much to deal with and I was hurt and out of work. After my wife and I sat down with one of the attorneys at The O'Connell Law Firm, all I had to worry about was getting better."
Mike E., Aurora, CO

We work with injured people every day, and we understand how devastating an accident can be. Our clients come to us with all types of serious injuries, from broken bones to chronic pain to brain damage. Unfortunately sometimes people don't survive their injuries, and we often have to handle claims resulting from the wrongful death of a loved one. In every case we take, injuries were the result of someone else's carelessness. Some of our clients will have to live with these injuries for the rest of their lives. In addition to the physical pain and trauma, the unfairness of this situation is often very difficult emotionally. The last thing that somebody who has been seriously injured in an accident wants to deal with is all the details of an insurance claim.

Many clients and their families also begin to have serious financial problems as time goes on. With any serious injury, medical bills can quickly add up, placing a strain on any household. We make sure that the injured person isn't hurt twice — once in the accident and again in the financial aftermath.

Some people are uncomfortable with the thought of asking for money to compensate them for injuries. They believe that no amount of money will reverse an injury or bring back a loved one. That's true, but unfortunately the system we have is the only one that can help at all. We have yet to meet a single client who wouldn't give back all the money if it could erase their injuries. We feel strongly that to be injured in an accident, and then to not be compensated, is to be injured twice.

Damages and Your Case: The Key to Compensation

"They found every dollar that there was. Our problem was that the person who hit us didn't have any insurance. That didn't stop our law firm. They found enough insurance to get us a fair settlement." Kellie G., Denver, CO

The justice system allocates money to accident victims based on their damages; in other words, the injuries and losses they have suffered as a result of the other person's wrongdoing. You'll read more about this in Chapter Two, but you should know for now that your damages can be roughly divided into two categories: economic damages, for financial costs related to the accident, and non-economic damages, for intangible but very real losses like pain and suffering that result from injuries. To collect money for those damages, you will usually have to prove to an insurance company or a jury that you suffered them.

All of this brings us to an important point: If we take your case, it means we think you have a strong claim, but no reputable lawyer will guarantee specific results. We can promise that we will work our very hardest to get you the best possible financial settlement or verdict. We have a strong record of past successes and have managed many, many claims to excellent conclusions.

Contingent Fees and Lower Costs

"I'm a college student and didn't have any money for an attorney, but thankfully that didn't matter. I got a great settlement and never had to worry about where I was going to find the money." Natalya M., Highlands Ranch, CO

Our early, aggressive representation is possible because of the type of fee we charge, a contingent fee. Like almost all reputable personal injury firms, we never charge a fee at the beginning of the case. Instead, we are paid a percentage of the money we recover for you when you settle or win the case. The percentage changes depending on when it settles, but it will always be explained to you *before* you agree to hire us. If you lose or for some reason your case cannot be settled, we will not ask for any legal fees at all. It's that simple. This allows us to represent everyone who comes to us with a strong case, regardless of their income or background. We also keep our costs low. Every dime we spend is carefully calculated to make sure it increases the value of your claim.

Cases We Handle: They Have Lawyers, You Should Too

This book is focused on the most common case we handle: automobile accidents. However, we handle a wide variety of cases arising from all types of serious accidents. Usually most of the issues that automobile accident clients have to deal with also apply to other types of accidents. So if you have been in an accident caused by negligence, we can probably help. We handle many types of cases, including:

Auto Accidents	Pedestrian Injuries	Semi Accidents
Motorcycle Accidents	Animal Bites	Catastrophic Injuries
Wrongful Death	Head and Brain Injuries	Nursing Home Abuse
Bad Faith Claims	Uninsured Motorist Claims	Slip and Fall cases

What all the situations listed in the table have in common is that they all result from negligence and carelessness. We can help an injured person in any of these situations. They do have differences and nuances, so the sooner you talk to an attorney, the better for you.

Insurance Companies: Profits Over People

"At first I thought I didn't need an attorney because I could handle my claim myself. It didn't take long to figure out that insurance companies do this for a living. The O'Connell Law Firm helped us level the playing field." - Janice T., Golden, CO

Insurance companies are not your friends. They may not actively wish you any harm, but their primary goal in the claims process is to save money by avoiding the need to pay you any more than necessary. This is the very nature of a profit-driven corporation with shareholders and a bottom line. You might say that their business oriented mission results in profits over people.

When insurance claims adjusters begin working on a claim, they will crunch the numbers and come up with a range of values that they believe should adequately compensate you. Typically, they will then make you an offer from the low end of that range. They rely on people's politeness, fear of bargaining or lack of knowledge regarding their rights to keep them from negotiating. An unrepresented party can reach an agreement with the insurance company that may not be fair, but at least the process will be over with.

Victims of serious injuries are unlikely to even do that well, however, because serious injuries tend to be very expensive, complicated, and take some time to fully understand and appreciate. They may even be life changing. After a serious accident, representatives from insurance companies have been known to contact accident victims within days or weeks to discuss a settlement. They might offer victims a small amount of money, ask them to sign or record something, or pressure them to settle right away, before they have time to learn the full extent of their injuries.

Frequently, insurers have been known to simply deny expensive claims that should be covered. They may use technicalities or half-truths, or simply accuse you of being mistaken about how the accident happened. Often they make an extremely low offer, and count on the fear people have of going to court or otherwise asserting their rights. We understand that fighting an insurance company or going to court to protect your rights is not what most people feel comfortable doing. That's why we're here. The other side has lawyers, you should too.

Colorado Law: The Rules of the Road

"I thought that the issues involved in a hit and run accident were straightforward. They're not— we really needed help." Terri K., Lakewood, CO

Colorado is what's called a tort state. This means that if you are injured in an accident caused by another driver, all compensation, including payment for medical bills, out-of-pocket expenses, lost wages, future medical expenses, and pain and suffering, must come from the driver who was at fault. As of 2009, a small portion of your medical expenses may be paid by your own policy under the "medical payments" provision. The fact that the at-fault driver's insurance should pay for almost all injuries and losses is an important one. It is critical to understand that the "other guy's" insurance company doesn't owe you anything. They don't have to be fair, they don't have to treat you with respect, and they don't even have to make you an offer to settle your claim. They are adverse to your interests. Their goal is to pay as little as possible to make you go away.

You need to take prompt action when you have been in a motor vehicle accident. This will help you preserve your rights as you seek proper compensation. An attorney can be the most important professional you'll ever speak with.

We Get Results

"By the time we decided to talk to an attorney, the insurance company had already made an offer that was just too low. Once my lawyer got involved I didn't even have to talk to the insurance company anymore, and my settlement doubled. Talking to Mr. O'Connell was one of the smartest things I could have done." Debbie A., Evergreen, CO

While every case is unique, the following three case studies illustrate how difficult even a seemingly straightforward accident can be, and how a law firm such as ours can help you through virtually any problem that arises after the accident has happened.

Jeff W.

Jeff W. was driving his pickup truck in the center lane, proceeding through a green light. Without warning, a car traveling in the opposite direction made a left turn directly into the path of Jeff's vehicle. When the cars collided, Jeff felt a sharp pain in his neck that traveled down his left arm and into his fingers.

When the police showed up, the driver making the left turn was given a ticket, but she also told the police that she thought Jeff's pickup truck was "going a little fast." The at-fault driver's insurance company picked up on this and claimed that Jeff contributed to the accident and they wouldn't pay full value. In the meantime, Jeff's neck got much worse and he needed surgery to fix the problem. What seemed like an open-and-shut case had become a difficult case. Jeff did the smart thing. He got on the Internet and began researching the issues, and determined that he needed help.

The lawyers at The O'Connell Law Firm knew what to do because they had seen it before. When an insurance company makes a bogus claim of comparative negligence (saying that Jeff was partially to blame), they are usually hoping to settle for a fraction of what the claim is worth. Unfortunately, for people without legal help, this often works.

We filed a lawsuit immediately, essentially daring the insurance company to prove their comparative negligence claim in court. They thought better of it, and the claim settled for $405,000, a fair value for this type of injury.

Brett R.

Brett's first attorney had dropped his case because he didn't like some of the facts, and didn't think it would be worth his while. Brett had been driving a motorcycle, when he was struck by a car that had run a stop sign, fracturing his femur in several places. The problem was that the motorcycle was borrowed, was uninsured, and Brett did not have a motorcycle license. No case, right? Not so fast.

Colorado law was firmly on Brett's side, and the attorneys at The O'Connell law Firm knew it immediately. The status of Brett's license, insurance status and ownership of the bike were completely irrelevant in this accident. The only things that mattered were the negligence of the other driver, and the fact that Brett was injured. On the second day of trial, the case settled for $250,000.

Michele C.

Michele was stopped at a red light on her way home where she lived with her parents, when she was rear-ended by a drunk driver. Michele sustained a concussion as well as back and neck injuries. To make matters worse, the guy who hit her didn't have insurance. Our lawyers quickly determined that since the at fault driver was uninsured, Michele was entitled to coverage under her policy, which was a Colorado minimum $25,000. Not enough. The legal team then determined that because Michele lived with her parents, under the "resident relative" principle, her parents' policy would "stack" on Michele's policy for added coverage. In the end, we were able to settle Michele's claim for $125,000, despite the fact that she was injured by an uninsured drunk driver.

Next Steps

"They treated us with respect and they were always there.'" Jeffrey M., Greeley, CO

We wrote this book hoping it would be a resource for people who suddenly find themselves dealing with the difficult physical, emotional and financial fallout from a serious accident. We hope it gives you a good grounding in personal injury law, and answers enough of your questions to get you going.

We know that no book can answer all the questions you might have. Every case is different, and every client will have questions that can only be answered after we learn more about his or her unique situation. That's why we'd like to invite you to come in and talk to us more about your case. We offer free, confidential initial consultations. During these meetings, we discuss your case and its prospects for a successful result. If you're not able to travel right now, we can bring this meeting to you, whether that means your home or any place that's convenient for you.

At the consultation, you can tell us exactly what happened and show us any documentation you might have. Then, we can give you our professional opinion about your case, and what we need to do to get you on your way to fair compensation. This consultation is also a job interview of sorts, meaning that it's your chance to interview us. Please don't be afraid to ask us, or any other law firm, questions about our style, staff, network of health-care providers or other things that might be important to you. We know hiring a lawyer is an important decision, and we want to be chosen on our merits.

If you want to set up a consultation, or if you just have questions, comments or concerns, we encourage you to contact us.

The O'Connell Law Firm, P.C.
I-25 and Colorado Blvd.
Denver, Colorado
phone: 303-759-4000 fax: 888-812-3375
www.ColoradoInjuryAttorney.net.

CHAPTER ONE

INSURANCE

Even people who have never been in a serious accident often dislike dealing with insurance companies. If you have been in an accident and have a large or complicated claim to make, you may soon find out why. Unfortunately, talking to insurance companies is an essential part of recovering from your accident, and how you handle these interactions can make or break your case. In this chapter, we have tried to present some of the basic information you need to make your insurance claims as successful as possible — even when the insurer causes problems.

Are You Covered?

After an accident, one of your first concerns will probably be whether your injuries and property damage are covered by auto insurance. Luckily, you probably have at least some insurance coverage, because 48 states make auto insurance mandatory. (The other two, Wisconsin and New Hampshire, allow residents to drive without insurance as long as they have the financial resources to pay for any damage they cause in an accident.) Unfortunately, having *some* auto insurance is not the same as having *enough* auto insurance — and some drivers break the law by carrying none at all. This is bad news if you rely on the other driver's insurance policy to cover your injuries.

Before we go on, you should understand how insurance works in your state. There are two types of auto insurance systems in the United States, and which one you use usually depends on where you live. Most states are at-fault or tort states, which means the other driver is legally responsible for any injuries and financial costs caused by the accident. Colorado is a tort state, as are most states in the country. The other driver's insurance policy is supposed to pay those costs, but you may have to sue to get payment if the facts are in dispute.

As of late 2008, eleven states (including New York and Florida) and Puerto Rico have no-fault auto insurance systems. Colorado was such a state until 2003 when the legislature changed the law to a tort (at-fault) system. If your insurance policy is called Personal Injury Protection (PIP), you probably live in a no-fault state. In a no-fault system, your own insurance company pays the costs of your injuries, no matter whose fault it was. In exchange for that security, you cannot file a lawsuit over the accident unless you meet certain qualifications. In some states, your financial costs must be above a certain amount; in others, your injuries must be very serious (as defined by law).

Three states have "choice no-fault" systems, which means each individual may choose either an at-fault policy or a no-fault (PIP) policy. As of late 2008, those states are New Jersey, Pennsylvania and Kentucky. If you are not sure what type of insurance you have, check your policy or ask your insurance adjuster.

Contacting Your Insurance Company

After you receive medical care and recover from the immediate effects of your accident, one of the first things you should do is call your insurance company. If you live in an at-fault state, you will probably also have to call the other driver's insurance company. You should make that call as soon as you reasonably can, because waiting too long might make it look to the insurance company like you are exaggerating your injuries. Calling quickly is also part of your obligations under the contract you signed with your insurer.

This first call should be fairly short. Its purpose is only to give the insurance adjuster the basic facts about your accident and the information for the other driver's insurance company, if there is one. In fact, during the call, the insurance adjuster on the other end should never ask to record you or ask you to sign anything, especially in exchange for money. If you get this kind of request, you may be dealing with a dishonest company; you should politely decline and call a lawyer as soon as possible.

During your initial call, the insurance adjuster will probably ask you who was at fault for the accident or who was to blame. He or she might also ask if anyone got a ticket. If this is disputed or you truly are not sure, just stick with the facts. During this or any other conversation with an insurer, it is important to avoid apologizing or accepting blame just to be polite, because that could be taken as an admission of guilt. And if you were knocked unconscious or taken to the hospital, you may not have gotten the full story. One way to get it is to get a copy of the accident report, if there is one, made by the police. If they will not release it, your insurance adjuster can get it for you and use it to start your claim.

UNDERSTANDING INSURANCE LAW CAN MAKE THE DIFFERENCE

Often, a more detailed understanding of insurance law can mean the difference in receiving full compensation for your injuries. Take, for example, the case of a 25-year-old day laborer who was seriously injured as a passenger on his way to the lake with a few of his friends. His injuries were severe and permanent, rendering him unable to work anymore. The other driver was clearly at fault, since he rear-ended the vehicle the young man was riding in. That driver's liability insurance carrier said there was a total of $30,000 on his policy, so the young man would not be able to recover any more compensation for his significant injuries.

The young man consulted several lawyers who declined his case, saying there was limited coverage (the $30,000) and his bills already exceeded $137,000. Then, the young man spoke to a friend who referred him to an experienced personal injury lawyer. That lawyer determined that while the vehicle the young man was riding in did not have underinsured motorist coverage, the trailer it was pulling did have coverage through his friend's father, a small business owner with a commercial insurance policy. The lawyer was convinced that there was underinsured motorist coverage through this policy, allowing his client to collect the full amount of his injuries. The lawyer negotiated and "worked" the case for over a year, finally convincing the insurance carrier that this client could collect on $1 million in additional insurance coverage.

The lawyer was able to settle the case for the limits of the trailer's commercial policy and structure this additional settlement in a special needs trust, which allowed the young man to keep receiving Medicaid and still buy a specially equipped house and car. By fully investigating the case and understanding insurance law, the lawyer was able to fully compensate the young man and provide for his future medical and financial needs.

How Do You Get Your Medical Bills Paid?

If you received any sort of medical treatment after the accident, you will have to worry about medical bills and health insurance claims as well as auto insurance claims. Auto insurance should cover your medical treatment, but hospitals prefer not to wait to work out who was at fault. If you were not able to give them your health insurance information (if any) when you arrived, they will probably try to bill you personally. You or your lawyer should be able to get the bill sent to the appropriate party later.

If you have both medical and auto insurance, you may be wondering which will pay for your medical costs. Under at-fault insurance plans, like those in Colorado, the hospital will start by billing you personally or billing the medical insurance company whose information you provide. Later, after you make your auto insurance claim, you or your health insurer may be reimbursed by the other driver's auto insurer. If you are among the drivers who have medical payment coverage on your auto insurance policy, your own insurance company may reimburse you.

If you have no-fault insurance (PIP coverage), your auto insurance company should pay. The hospital may bill you personally at first, especially if you could not provide them with insurance information when you arrived, but it should be simple to transfer the obligation to your insurer. You may still have a deductible under your PIP policy. If your bills are higher than the amount of PIP coverage you have, any medical insurance will take over after your auto insurance coverage is used up.

If there are problems, keep in mind that most states ultimately hold you responsible for your own medical bills, regardless of whether insurance should cover it. That means you should take action quickly if the insurance company refuses to meet its obligations.

Auto Repairs and Other Property Damage

If you were injured in your accident, the chances are good that there was also damage to your property. Damage to your car, truck or other vehicle is the most common type of property damage, but any other property you lost or had to repair because of the accident should also qualify. The same auto insurance policy that covers your injuries should also cover all of your property damage.

Generally, claims of damage to your vehicle fall into two categories. If the insurance company says your car or truck is "totaled," it means the repair costs are likely to be greater than the actual fair market value of the vehicle. That makes it not worth repairing, at least to the insurance company. (You are free to do what you like with a "totaled" vehicle.) The fair market value of the vehicle is determined by its age, condition, mileage, appearance, depreciation and other factors. Each insurer does this differently, and some take into account incidental costs like storage.

Because car loans and other financial obligations related to the vehicle are not considered in determining fair market value, your car or truck might be considered worth less than what you owe for it. This is especially likely with newer vehicles, which depreciate (lose value) quickly within their first few years of use. The insurance company is obligated to pay only the actual cash value of the vehicle immediately prior to the accident, not the cost of repairs you made or your original purchase price. A special type of insurance called gap insurance is designed for this situation; it pays the difference between actual cash value and any loans you still owe. Gap insurance is optional, but insurers will probably try to sell it to owners of new vehicles.

If the insurance company considers the vehicle repairable, it should pay for repairs by a body shop or a mechanic. Your insurance coverage may pay for your use of a rental car during repairs, or compensate you for the temporary loss of your car or truck. Some states allow you to choose your own repair shop; others allow the insurance company to choose. If you disagree with the insurance company's estimation of the damage, you can sometimes get a second opinion from another repair shop.

Dealing With Uninsured and Underinsured Drivers

If you were hit by an uninsured or underinsured driver, you have an especially difficult task ahead. An uninsured driver is a driver with no insurance coverage at all; an underinsured driver is one with some coverage, but not enough to cover the damage he or she caused. (A hit-and-run driver is considered an uninsured motorist, at least until he or she can be identified.) In a no-fault state, your own PIP coverage should cover at least some of your injuries and property damage. But in an at-fault state, being hit by an uninsured or underinsured driver may mean there is no money at all available to cover your injuries. You are free to sue, of course, but most individuals are not wealthy enough to fully pay for a serious injury.

In at-fault states, and in no-fault states with low coverage limits, more and more drivers are responding to this risk by carrying uninsured/underinsured motorist insurance that supplements their basic policies. In fact, some states require it. Uninsured/underinsured motorist coverage compensates you for the costs of the accident, up to the limits of the uninsured/underinsured policy. Unfortunately, the actual cost of your injuries can still exceed those limits. And because uninsured/underinsured motorist claims can be difficult to document, some insurance companies make them difficult to collect.

INSURANCE MAY COVER YOU, EVEN WITH AN UNINSURED DRIVER

If you were hit by a driver without insurance in an at-fault state, you may think you are out of luck — unable to collect any settlement at all. But before you give up, you should always call an experienced personal injury lawyer. The experienced personal injury lawyer is sure to look at all possibilities for insurance coverage, including insurance covering the driver, the vehicle's owner, and any user given permission to use the vehicle, as well as a client's own insurance coverage, before giving up.

In one case, a law firm was able to help a distraught woman who was hit by an uninsured driver in an at-fault state. This driver was clearly at fault for the accident. In fact, he said at the scene that he knew he was at fault, but had no insurance to pay for the damage. The client had purchased collision coverage only, thinking she was doing the smart thing by saving money. Because neither driver had any insurance that applied to the crash, this woman thought she was out of luck. Still, she called a law firm, which agreed to take her case.

After investigating the facts, the law firm discovered that the at-fault driver was driving his girlfriend's mother's vehicle — with the permission of his girlfriend to run an errand. Also, as it turned out, the mother and daughter had an agreement that the daughter could borrow her mother's car as needed from time to time. That meant the at-fault driver was a "permissive user" under the policy— someone who has permission to drive the car — which meant that he was covered by the mother's liability insurance. In most states, liability coverage will cover permissive users of an insured automobile. This was true even though the driver of both vehicles involved in the accident were personally uninsured.

This scenario is actually quite common. Although laws in almost every state require all drivers to have liability insurance, many violate the law. An experienced personal injury lawyer may be able to help by searching thoroughly for an applicable insurance policy covering any party involved in the accident.

When a Disability Takes You Out of Work

If your injuries take you out of work for more than a few days, you stand to lose a lot of wages. If you have short-term or long-term disability coverage (under auto insurance or separately), you should be able to collect payments that help you make ends meet while you are out of work. If you are eligible for this coverage and decide to use it, you may hear from your insurance company about "subrogation," which is a legal term for transferring the obligation to pay from one party to another. (You can find more about subrogation in Chapter Six.) In an at-fault state, subrogation gives your disability insurer the right to be reimbursed if you win any money for lost wages from a third party, such as the insurance company for the other driver. Because this can be complex, your lawyer should handle it for you.

You may be entitled to payment of lost wages from your own PIP insurer in a no-fault state. Because you do not necessarily need to sue, subrogation is limited in no-fault states, and it is handled differently in each state. Again, your lawyer should handle this for you.

Dealing With Workers' Compensation Insurance

If you were at work during your accident, you are probably entitled to workers' compensation benefits. Workers' compensation pays the cost of any injuries you sustain at work and a limited replacement wage while you are unable to work, regardless of who was at fault for the injury. Your employer carries workers' compensation insurance to cover those payments. In exchange for collecting them, you agree not to sue your employer, even if you believe it caused the accident. However, if a third party was responsible for the injury, you may still be able to sue that party while collecting workers' compensation benefits. Subrogation may also come into play with a workers' compensation case, because multiple insurance companies are often involved in a claim.

Workers' compensation law is a complicated area that depends largely on the laws of your state, and many lawyers focus their practice on it completely. Many workers have trouble collecting workers' compensation because replacement wages can be expensive — and insurance companies prefer not to pay expensive claims, even when they are legally obligated to. If you have a workers' compensation claim as a result of your accident, your lawyer may refer that part of your case to another lawyer who specializes in workers' compensation law.

Settling Your Claim With the Insurance Adjuster

Sometimes, it is possible to settle an accident claim by just working with the insurance adjuster. This is most likely when you have few injuries that require little medical treatment, or no injuries at all. In this situation, you may not even need help from a lawyer. But before you close your claim, you should make sure you have identified all of your injuries and property damage and feel that you will be truly fully compensated by the payments you will receive.

Most people do not realize that they are not required to take the first settlement their insurance companies offer. In fact, you are allowed to negotiate for the fullest compensation you are entitled to, using documentation from police, repair shops and other independent parties to support your claim. But if your insurer refuses to change its offer, a lawyer can drastically change your situation. Hiring a lawyer to handle the negotiations lets the insurer know that you know your rights and are prepared to enforce them, if necessary.

The Adjuster Is Not Your Friend

Because we refer to "our" insurance companies, it can be easy to believe that insurance adjusters are here to help us. Unfortunately, that is just not true. Insurance companies are in business to make money, and premiums — the monthly or yearly payments we make to have insurance — are just part of their profit. Like any other business, insurers make more money if they keep costs low. In an insurance company's case, that means paying less to people with expensive claims. The job of an insurance adjuster is to save the company money by settling your claim for as little money as possible.

If you were seriously injured in your accident, you may not be in the best position to fight with your insurance company. Hiring a lawyer may be the best decision you can make to protect yourself, your family and your future.

CHAPTER TWO

UNDERSTANDING YOUR INJURIES AND DAMAGES

In personal injury law, the wrongdoer (sometimes known as a tortfeasor) is responsible for all of the injuries caused by his or her negligence, or by any other unlawful conduct. If you are injured as a direct result of that conduct, you are entitled to be fully compensated for all the injuries that you suffered. In the law, the goal is to make the injured party whole. That is, the purpose of monetary compensation is to try to restore you and your family to the position that you were in before your accident.

Once it is clear that the wrongdoer is at fault for the accident, an experienced personal injury lawyer can help you fully identify and understand your injuries. Your law firm will obtain and review your medical records and talk with you, your family and even your physicians to fully understand your injuries and how they have affected your life. Using prior experience with similar cases, your lawyer will then be able to predict the range of dollar amounts a jury could award.

In recent years, insurance companies, their lobbyists and greedy corporations have put forth a great deal of propaganda that casts personal injury victims and their lawyers in an unfavorable light. They do this purposely to bias potential jurors against personal injury victims and in favor of the people and insurance companies they sue. Often, the media exacerbates this problem by highlighting bizarre or rare multi-million-dollar cases. This creates the mistaken perception that most people pursuing personal injury claims receive unjust windfalls, or do not entirely deserve the compensation they receive. Nothing is further from the truth. In reality, most people injured by careless wrongdoers are hardworking Americans who just happened to be in the wrong place at the wrong time.

PROVING YOUR INJURIES CAN PROVE YOUR CLAIM

Sometimes, understanding your injuries can actually help prove your case. Take the case of a 9-year-old boy who was hit by a car while running back across the street from an ice cream truck. The driver of the car claimed that she was not at fault and that the boy had simply run into the side of the car. Even the investigating police officer took the driver's word and decided the little boy was at fault. There were no other witnesses.

However, thanks to the experienced personal injury lawyer the boy's family consulted, that was not the end of the investigation. The lawyer investigated and researched the particular type of leg fracture the boy had. To make a long story short, the lawyer was able to prove, using medical and scientific evidence and testimony, that the only way the injury could have occurred was if the car had hit the boy, as opposed to the boy running into the car. By fully understanding the injuries in the case, the lawyer was able to turn a claim denied by the insurance company into a substantial recovery to provide for the boy's future.

Follow Through With Your Doctors

The full extent of your injuries may not be obvious immediately after an accident. Some people may feel that they did not sustain a serious injury, only to discover weeks or months later that what they initially thought was a minor injury has worsened and may require significant medical treatment. Because of this possibility, one of the things you should do after an accident is see a doctor for a full evaluation. Depending on the type of injury, it may be best to consult with a specialist. Be certain to tell your doctor about all of your symptoms, no matter how minor they may seem. You should see this doctor as soon as possible after your accident, so the doctor can properly document the full extent of your injuries. This documentation is important because it creates a clear record of your injuries and treatment, which is essential in a legal claim.

MEDICAL RECORDS CAN BE ESSENTIAL

One example of a case in which understanding the injuries was crucial was the case of a 50-year-old construction worker, who suffered back injuries after being struck by a dropped piece of drywall. The worker had been employed in the construction industry for 30 years at the time of his accident, and had back pain on and off throughout his working life, just because of the nature of his job. Thankfully, he was always able to recover from whatever was causing his back pain and return to work without restrictions.

In this case, the drywall was dropped by an employee from another company. That company contended that the injured worker's back problems were preexisting, so they were not responsible for the injury. However, after a thorough investigation, the injured worker's lawyer was able to prove that the back injuries were new and truly were caused by the falling drywall. The lawyer used medical evidence such as a detailed comparison of imaging studies taken before and after the accident, consultation with medical experts and further medical testing to prove when the injuries occurred. This proof made the difference in the case, allowing the injured worker to recover financial compensation for his medical care, his pain and other damages.

Immediately after the accident, it may be difficult even for the most experienced doctor to tell you how long you will require medical treatment. Depending on your injuries, you may need follow-up care for the first few weeks or months after you leave the hospital. For some extremely serious injuries, you may need long-term or even lifelong care. Because it is often difficult to predict your needs early in a case, it is important for you to be vigilant about your health. If you notice a change in your symptoms, you should be certain to tell your doctor about it. You should also, of course, actively participate in your own recovery by following your doctor's orders, taking your medications and undergoing whatever rehabilitation or treatment your doctor recommends.

Your lawyer will also need to know about changes in your condition and how they affect your life, so he or she can explain the full extent of your injuries and damages to the insurance company and ask for the fairest settlement of your claim. To help your lawyer, you should keep a written record of your medical treatment and how your life has been affected by your injuries. This will also help you refresh your memory later, in case your claim goes to trial months or years after the accident.

When your treatment is completed or your doctor feels you have reached maximum medical improvement, your lawyer may request additional medical records, to better understand how the injuries will affect you in the future.

Types of Injuries

Under the law, a personal injury is any harm that you as an individual sustain, including physical injuries, financial costs and emotional trauma. Injuries can also be personal losses, such as losing the care and companionship of a loved one.

As you work to resolve your accident claim, you may hear insurance adjusters, lawyers and doctors talk about different degrees of injuries. You may hear injuries described as minor, moderate, severe or catastrophic. Minor or moderate injuries can be injuries such as sprains, strains, fractures, bruising or superficial cuts. These may be painful, but they usually heal well and quickly, with minimal medical treatment.

You may hear insurance adjusters refer to "soft tissue injuries." Soft tissue injuries are injuries to the non-bony parts of the body, such as internal organs, nerves, muscles and connective tissues. Sprains, whiplash and pulled muscles are all types of soft tissue injuries. Even if you have a bruise over the affected area, you and your doctor may not realize you have a soft tissue injury under the bruise, because it can be hidden from sight and hard to detect with tests. Soft tissue injuries may heal quickly, but they can also take a long time to heal. Some can even result in chronic pain and disability, which can be permanent if not treated properly. Typically, it is harder to recover substantial compensation in these cases than in cases involving serious or catastrophic injuries.

A catastrophic injury is a serious injury that is expected to permanently change the victim's life. Examples of this type of injury include burns, amputations, spinal cord injuries, paralysis and head injuries (also called traumatic brain injuries). These types of injuries result in the most significant settlements and verdicts, because the injuries can be proven objectively and are more obvious to the insurance company or the jurors.

Although catastrophic injuries are immediately obvious in most cases, sometimes the full extent of the injury is not immediately revealed. This is especially true when the victim suffered a traumatic brain injury, which may also be called a closed head injury. In some cases, the brain may be affected in ways so subtle that only people close to the victim notice changes in abilities, behavior or personality. A closed head injury can be caused by physical trauma (a hard blow or penetrating wound), a blast wave from an explosion or violent shaking of the head. It often results from actual jostling of the brain. Such trauma can damage the tissues of the brain, which in turn affects the abilities controlled by the damaged tissue.

A concussion is the mildest form of brain injury, but more serious brain injuries leave their victims permanently disabled. Naturally, brain injuries affect many aspects of the injured person's life, including physical movement, the senses, intellectual ability, creativity and even personality. Sometimes, what appears to be a minor concussion or brief loss of consciousness following a car accident can result in a serious closed head injury, with symptoms such as chronic headaches, memory loss, loss of concentration or changes in a person's personality or behavior.

Permanent Disability

Unfortunately, some people's injuries lead to permanent disabilities, either partial or total. A permanent disability is any loss of ability that will affect the rest of the victim's life, and at least partially impair his or her ability to work or perform other day-to-day activities.

A permanent disability is often a major, life-changing event for victims and their families. In addition to the disability itself, disabled accident victims also face a higher risk of medical complications than uninjured people and often suffer profound emotional injuries because of their disabilities. People with permanent disabilities may require significant medical help, such as home health care nurses, extensive inpatient medical care and rehabilitation or long-term accommodation in an assisted living facility. Someone who has suffered a permanent disability is much more likely to recover a large judgment than someone who has fully recovered.

Medical Expenses

As everyone who lives in a modern society knows, health care can be very expensive. Even if you have medical insurance or good medical coverage through an auto insurance policy, you may be charged thousands or tens of thousands of dollars for a lengthy hospital stay, a trip to a specialized care center or repeated doctor visits and physical therapy appointments. If you do not have medical insurance, these costs can quickly reach into five or six figures. For someone who has suffered a catastrophic injury or a permanent disability, lifelong medical treatment can cost millions of dollars.

In a personal injury claim, these medical expenses are part of the damages (financial compensation) you are entitled to claim. This is not limited to direct health care costs, but may extend to any medical expense, including prescriptions, medical devices and the cost of transportation to and from your doctor's office. Recovering your medical expenses is an essential element of your personal injury claim.

If your case involves a catastrophic injury, your lawyer will want to not only determine your existing medical costs, but also hire medical experts to determine the likely cost of your future medical treatment. In some cases, your law firm may need to hire an expert to develop a "life care plan" that predicts all of your future medical needs. This expert will evaluate your injuries, review your medical records and project the cost of future medical care.

Lost Income and Loss of Earning Capacity

If you are unable to work because of your injuries, you are entitled to claim the income you lose. In addition, if you have a disability that affects your future earning potential, you are also entitled to recover monetary damages for loss of the income you would otherwise have earned.

For example, let us say that you can no longer do the specific job you had at the time of the accident, but you find a job within your physical limitations that pays less than your previous job. In this case, you would be entitled to recover not only the income you lost from the old job, but also any future income you lose because you had to take the lower-paying job. If you are self-employed and your injury makes you unable to do your job, you may need to hire someone to replace you. You may be entitled to compensation for the extra money you pay to that person during your recovery.

In addition to your lost income and loss of future earning capacity, you may be entitled to recover any loss of benefits, such as health insurance, pension plans, bonuses or other benefits directly associated with your employment. An experienced personal injury lawyer will help you determine all of your financial losses so you can seek compensation for those losses. Your lawyer may need to hire experts, such as a vocational expert (an expert in work) or an economist. These experts will review your financial and medical records, then calculate and predict the economic losses you have suffered from the accident. If you are self-employed, you can prove your economic losses through tax returns and other business documents.

Pain and Suffering Damages

Another part of your personal injury claim is the way your injuries affect your daily life — your pain and suffering. Personal injury victims are entitled to recover damages for past and present suffering as well as any suffering they may experience in the future. These damages for pain and suffering are different types of damages from those you would claim for your economic losses or physical injuries. For example, someone who suffers chronic pain after an injury is entitled to be compensated for that pain and suffering.

Pain and suffering are not the same. Physical pain is a sensation and suffering is a mood. Pain is the awareness, through a stimulus in the brain, or something that could damage your tissues and is followed by a feeling of discomfort or unpleasantness. By contrast, suffering is an emotion that could be considered the opposite of happiness or enjoyment, and involves cognitive awareness of an unpleasant situation, or a lack of the pleasure the victim could have expected had it not been for the accident. Suffering could involve many emotions, including depression, anxiety and humiliation. For example, suffering could be embarrassment and anxiety from a disfiguring facial injury, an amputation, incontinence, paralysis or another injury that severely limits the victim's life activities.

It is the job of an experienced personal injury lawyer to help you prove specifically how your injuries have affected your life and your family. The ultimate goal of a personal injury claim is to obtain the maximum possible compensation, so you may return to your life as it was before the accident. Although injuries make that impossible in some cases, you are entitled to seek compensation for every injury you suffer. It is the goal of a personal injury lawyer to help you obtain the fullest and fairest compensation permitted by the law.

Loss of Consortium

In many states, the law allows the spouse of an injured person to recover damages as well, even if the spouse was not injured. This is called a loss of consortium claim.

Black's Law Dictionary defines "consortium" as the "conjugal fellowship of husband and wife, and the right of each to the company, society, and cooperation, affection and aid of the other in every conjugal relation." Loss of consortium includes not only material services that you may lose because of a spouse's injury, but such intangibles as society, guidance, companionship and sexual relations. Usually, you may only make a loss of consortium claim when one spouse has been seriously injured, and that injury has had a direct negative effect on the marital relationship. Generally, you cannot make a loss of consortium claim if you are merely living with the injured person. A marital relationship is essential to making a loss of consortium claim.

Often, the non-injured spouse, at the direction of an experienced personal injury lawyer, can present compelling testimony at trial. This helps convince a jury that an accident has affected not only the marital relationship, but also the family. Juries can sometimes empathize with the spouse who was not injured and better appreciate how the injuries have affected the marriage and the family. An experienced personal injury lawyer can help you determine whether you should add a loss of consortium claim to your personal injury claim.

Common Defenses Used by Insurance Companies

As experienced personal injury lawyers, we have years of experience with the misrepresentations, exaggerations and outright lies insurance companies commonly use after injury victims make a legal claim. One common defense is to suggest that the victim suffered from similar injuries before the accident, or that the victim was predisposed to the type of injury he or she suffered. Yet another defense is to try to prove that the victim's injuries were not caused by the accident, but by other events in the victim's life. When insurance companies cannot dispute the fault of their insureds (customers), they might resort to the age-old tactic of attacking a plaintiff's character or preexisting medical history.

A good lawyer will successfully challenge these common defenses and help the victim present his or her injuries clearly, concisely and coherently. For example, even if you suffered from a similar medical problem (such as a back or neck condition) before the accident, your lawyer can help you prove that your previous injury was made worse as a result of your accident. Most state laws support the premise that a wrongdoer "takes his victim as he finds him." This means victims are entitled to recover full compensation even if they were particularly susceptible to an injury, or predisposed to experience greater pain or suffering than could have been foreseen by the defendant.

For example, you have a bad back that never required surgery, but then you are involved in a serious car accident that aggravates the back condition enough to require surgery, you are entitled to recover compensation for the surgery. After all, you would not have needed it if the accident had never happened.

Doctors and Other Medical Providers

If you have been seriously injured for the first time, you may be encountering types of doctors that you have never heard of before. The following are some of the medical specialists that personal injury victims are most likely to encounter.

An **anesthesiologist** administers drugs to provide pain relief during surgery. Some anesthesiologists also treat chronic pain. Anesthesiologists who treat pain are also sometimes called specialists in **pain management.**

A **burn specialist** is exactly what it sounds like — someone who cares for patients with severe burns.

A **dermatologist** handles diseases and injuries to the skin, including burns.

A **doctor of emergency medicine** usually works in an emergency room. This doctor may have been the first doctor to treat you after the accident.

The doctor you most likely see regularly is probably a **family practice** or **general practice doctor**. Depending on your injuries, he or she might take an active part in your care or refer you to a specialist.

A **neurologist** treats injuries and abnormalities of the nervous system, which includes the brain and spinal cord. This is the doctor you will see if you have a brain or spinal injury. If you need surgery, you might also see a **neurological surgeon** or **spinal surgeon**.

An **orthopedic doctor** treats injuries to the bones, muscles and joints, sometimes including amputations as well as broken bones.

A doctor who treats problems with joints is a **rheumatologist**.

For accident victims, doctors of **plastic surgery**, **reconstructive surgery** or **cosmetic surgery** work to correct damage to the body or unsightly scars, and to restore functions or prevent loss of functions.

Physical therapists and doctors of **physical medicine** and **rehabilitation** work with injury victims to restore movement or function to areas affected by an injury. This sometimes includes functions that you might not think of as physical, like brushing your teeth or writing.

Psychiatrists handle mental health issues, including emotional injuries caused by accidents.

Specialists in other specific parts of the body include **nephrologists** (kidneys), **hepatologists** (liver), **gastroenterologists** (the digestive system), **cardiologists** (heart), **pulmonary specialists** (lungs) and **podiatrists** (feet and ankles).

Common Medical Tests

If you sustained any sort of internal injury, including an injury to the spine, brain or internal organs, your doctor may ask you to take one of these special tests. This is good, because the more information you have about your injuries, the easier it will be to begin healing. This will also make it easier for your lawyer to prove your injuries. Tests you might take include:

X-rays are the radiation tests we are all familiar with; you have probably taken one at the dentist if you had your wisdom teeth removed. They show bony structures, so they are best for diagnosing bone injuries and cannot be used to diagnose soft tissue injuries.

A **CT scan**, sometimes known as a **CAT scan**, is short for "computerized tomography scan." A CT scan uses multiple x-rays taken in a circle around the same point to build a better picture than one x-ray could provide alone, using a computer to combine them. A CT scan is likely to be ordered if the doctors believe you have an injury to the internal organs of your torso or abdomen, or multiple fractures to a hand or foot.

MRI is short for magnetic resonance imaging. If you get an MRI, the doctors will ask you to lie down in a large tube that uses harmless magnetic radiation to look at soft tissues of the body. Sometimes they will also ask you to drink or have an injection of a substance that makes those tissues easier to see. If your doctor suspects an injury to your brain or spinal cord, you might be asked to do this test. Because this technology uses magnets, you cannot use it if you have a pacemaker or other metal implanted in your body.

A **PET scan** is often used in tandem with a CT scan. In a PET scan, the patient is injected with a harmless substance that can be seen by the scanner using radioactivity. Unlike CT scans, PET scans can show your body's metabolic activity rather than just structures of the body. The images they produce are also three-dimensional.

If you know anyone who has had a baby recently, you are probably familiar with an **ultrasound**. An ultrasound test uses high-frequency sound waves that bounce off internal structures of the body to build an image. The image it builds is not as detailed as images from other methods, but because it does not use radiation, it may be the best choice for people with certain conditions. It is also less expensive than an MRI. Doctors use it to look at internal organs, connective tissue, bones, blood vessels and eyes.

If your doctors believe you have a nerve injury, you may take a **nerve conduction study**, an electrical test that can detect problems with your nerves. In this test, one electrode is placed over the nerve being tested, while another is placed in a "downstream" area of the nervous system. The speed it takes for the electricity to travel between them determines whether there is nerve damage.

An **electromyograph** (EMG) shows muscles' activity by measuring the electrical current they produce when they are in motion. This might be used for people with nerve damage, muscle weakness or the conditions that might cause them. In an EMG, doctors either insert a thin needle into the muscle being tested or place an electrode over the area, then measure the electrical impulses of the muscle.

An **endoscopy** uses a flexible tube with a light and a camera to look inside natural openings in your body, such as the throat. This is most commonly associated with tests on the stomach or colon, but can be used in any area with a natural opening.

Health Care Facilities

If you are seriously injured, you may end up at a health care facility more specialized than the hospitals we are all used to. If you need this kind of care, you might even be transferred from your original hospital to one of these facilities:

A **trauma center** handles patients who have sustained a sudden and serious physical injury. They are ranked from Level I to Level IV, with the most serious cases at Level I facilities. Because they are expensive to run, they are not common; patients outside major cities may have to be airlifted to one.

A **rehabilitation center** is a facility where patients work to reestablish or relearn abilities they lost because of a serious injury, through therapy. **Physical therapy** helps with movement or prevents loss of movement, while **occupational therapy** might focus on relearning activities of daily life or finding ways to perform them despite a new disability.

Burn centers focus on patients with serious burns. They not only treat burn injuries, but work to help patients return to everyday life, often with therapists, social workers, psychiatrists and other professionals who are not conventional doctors.

Assisted living facilities may be appropriate for injury victims who need long-term physical or occupational therapy and help with everyday living. This might be true of someone with a severe brain injury or spinal damage. In addition to providing meals and housekeeping, as at a nursing home, the staff at an assisted living facility works with patients to help them regain independence and abilities. Some patients are able to return home eventually; others may need to remain in a facility throughout their lives.

Home care is an option for patients whose injuries do not require full-time hospitalization. A nurse or other health care professional might visit every day or a few times a week. Depending on the injuries, the professional might do anything from changing bandages to administering a treatment with an IV to helping with personal needs.

CHAPTER THREE

CHOOSING A LAWYER

The lawyer you choose is one of the most important factors in the success or failure of your case. It is a decision you should make with care. Unfortunately, choosing a lawyer can be intimidating for people who have never been through the process before. You may be justifiably concerned about ending up with a lawyer with bad ethics or poor skills. In this chapter, we hope to ease those fears and provide a basic guide to finding a personal injury lawyer.

The first thing to consider is that lawyers, much like doctors, often concentrate their practices in specific areas of the law. If you need hip replacement surgery, you would probably see an orthopedic surgeon, not a cardiologist. Similarly, if you are in an accident, you will not want to hire a lawyer who focuses on divorce. Another type of lawyer may be able to help you, but he or she will not have the same experience and skills that a personal injury lawyer brings to a personal injury case. Personal injury lawyers understand the legal, procedural and evidentiary strategies that can maximize the value of your personal injury claim, because they work with these issues every day.

At our firm, we find that many of our clients come to us after a recommendation from someone they know who has used us in the past.

You can also start by considering lawyer advertisements. You have probably seen lawyer ads on television, in newspapers or in the Yellow Pages. Consistent advertisements from a particular lawyer show that his or her firm has been practicing for all of that time, and is likely to have the experience and resources necessary to take on insurance companies. In fact, insurance companies sometimes decide whether or not they will settle a case before a trial based on the reputation and experience of your lawyer.

WHY HIRE A LAWYER?

The question may enter your mind: *Should I even hire a lawyer, as opposed to just dealing directly with the insurance company and its adjuster?* You should know that although the insurance adjuster may seem friendly and cooperative, he or she works for the insurance company that will pay to settle your claim. If the insurance adjuster can persuade you to settle your claim for less than what it is worth, that is good for the insurance company but bad for you. Unlike a lawyer you hire, the insurance company has no legal duty or financial incentive to treat you fairly!

Case in point: A working-class mother had a serious accident with a commercial tractor-trailer rig. She was injured in the accident and her car was so badly damaged that it was useless, both of which posed challenges for this mother of three young children. The very next day, she was visited at home by a representative from the truck driver's insurance company. The insurance adjuster was very skilled at creating a sense that he was there to help her deal with the problems the accident had caused. After learning that she had no medical insurance, he told her that he believed she would make a good recovery, based on his experience and the way she was able to get around in her home and carry one of her children. Based on this evaluation, he offered her cash to repair her damaged vehicle, and $1,000 to compensate her for the trouble and pain she may have experienced. All she needed to do was accept the cash that day and sign the release, barring her from making any further financial claim.

Although tempted, she called her husband at work. He told her not to accept or sign anything and to call a lawyer immediately. After contacting a lawyer, she eventually found that she had severe injuries to her shoulder and would need a period of treatment and testing to see if she could recover without surgery. Fortunately, she recovered without surgery after receiving the necessary treatment and was fairly and fully compensated for her months of suffering and damages. Ultimately, she received nearly 25 times what the adjuster wanted her to accept. As you can imagine, this client and her family were immensely pleased with their decision to retain a lawyer rather than deal directly with the insurance company.

Today many, if not most people turn to the internet for their searches. Using a search engine like Google, Yahoo! or MSN, you can easily search by both your location and the legal specialty you need. There are many ways to search for this information. Here are a few tips that may be helpful:

1. Search for a phrase instead of a single word. "Colorado auto accident lawyer" will probably turn up more useful results than just "lawyer."
2. Put the phrase you search for in quotes. This will tell the search engine to look for the entire phrase as you searched for it, not the individual words in the phrase. Without quotes, your results will be greater in number but not nearly as relevant to your search. Just make sure to spell everything correctly.
3. Narrow your search by including some geographical information. For example, if your auto accident happened in New York, you might want to search for "New York auto accident lawyer." You need a lawyer in the state where the accident happened, even if that is not the state where you live or have legal residency.

The Initial Consultation

When you first call a law firm, your call may be taken by a lawyer, a paralegal, a case manager or an intake specialist. This person will ask you for basic contact information, as well as the details of your accident. Based on your answers, a lawyer will make an initial assessment of your case and may schedule a consultation. If you cannot travel to the law firm, many personal injury lawyers are willing to have the consultation on the telephone, in your home or at the hospital. At our firm, we make every effort to accommodate clients and potential clients with this type of need.

During the initial consultation, you will be asked for details about your accident and your injuries. Because details can be hard to remember, and because some clients feel intimidated or stressed by this meeting, we recommend that clients bring all of the documents they have that are related to the accident — things like police reports, hospital bills, your insurance policy and more. We always do our best to put clients at ease and explain everything as thoroughly as possible, without "legalese."

Questions the lawyer is likely to ask at your consultation include:

1. Did anyone receive a ticket?
2. Was a police report made? If so, do you have a copy?
3. Did you take photos of the vehicle?
4. Did you take photos of your injuries?
5. Did you give a statement to police, insurance adjusters or anyone else?
6. Were there any witnesses, and if so, did anyone get their contact information?
7. How much damage was done to your vehicle?
8. What medical treatment have you had thus far?
9. What medical treatment, tests or follow-up are currently recommended by your treating physician(s)?
10. How are you feeling?
11. How are your bills being paid?
12. What insurance companies are involved?

Once you have discussed all of this, the lawyer should bring up his or her fees. Most personal injury lawyers work on what is called a contingency-fee basis. This means that you are not required to pay for legal services unless and until the case has been won. The lawyer should have a fee agreement that specifies that he or she will be paid with a percentage of the financial settlement or verdict. The size of that percentage depends on whether the claim is resolved before or after the lawsuit is filed. (It is possible, and common, to resolve claims before filing; see Chapter Four for more.)

This arrangement may sound strange, but it remains popular because it allows lawyers to take strong cases brought by clients who might not be able to afford legal fees otherwise. We believe this is an essential and valuable part of our legal system, providing access to justice for everyone, no matter what their income or background might be.

CHOOSE YOUR LAWYER CAREFULLY

Choosing the right lawyer can have a substantial effect on the results of your personal injury claim. An experienced personal injury lawyer who meets you and takes the time to listen carefully to the facts of your case can sometimes save you substantial financial and personal hardship. Take the case of a 39-year-old man who was hurt in an auto accident, who had already undergone one cervical spine surgery to correct injuries from his accident. To settle his claim, the insurance company had offered him just $150,000 out of a total available insurance policy of $250,000. What's more, the man did not realize that he had an additional $750,000 in underinsured motorist insurance, which could cover his treatment if his claim exceeded the $250,000 limit.

The man and his wife consulted several personal injury lawyers to discuss whether they should accept the insurance company's offer. The first two lawyers they consulted did not delve into all of his medical problems. Importantly, they did not identify the fact that he would likely require future surgeries, which could jeopardize his livelihood as a salesman who traveled thousands of miles a year. Fortunately, the couple sought out the advice of one of the experienced personal injury lawyers who wrote this book. After listening carefully to the prospective client, the lawyer realized that this gentleman was a likely candidate for future surgeries that could threaten his career. The lawyer recommended that he wait for several months before considering any settlement offers, in order to see whether he needed more treatment or had other problems related to the accident.

As the lawyer suspected, the man ultimately needed two additional cervical spine surgeries, which resulted in permanent physical limitations. He was terminated from his job and ultimately had to accept a job paying significantly less. Based on these lost future earnings and his additional surgeries, the lawyer was able to negotiate a settlement that was over six times the amount of the offer from the defendant's insurance carrier. In this case, waiting to make a claim until he fully understood his injuries and hiring an experienced personal injury lawyer, helped the man avoid the financial and medical problems that might have resulted from taking the smaller initial offer.

What Is the Next Step?

When you find the right lawyer, you will sign a contract formally retaining him or her as *your* lawyer, giving you all of the rights of a client. To get the case started, your lawyer may direct staffers to obtain your medical records, doctors' notes and medical test results, along with a copy of any accident report and any insurance information or statements the insurer might have recorded.

If necessary, the lawyer might also retain a private investigator to find important but elusive information about your case. All of this case development takes time. At our firm, we have found that clients really appreciate being kept informed, whether or not we have anything significant to report. For that reason, we assign specific staffers to update clients regularly about the status of their cases.

In this first stage, your lawyer is working to understand the facts and the strength of your case. After the case is built, your lawyer can begin negotiating with the other side to get you the best possible compensation under the laws of your state and the facts of your individual case. You may end up settling the case outside of court or participating in a full trial. You will learn more about this process, the stages of a lawsuit and your own responsibilities in Chapters Four through Seven.

What if My Case Is Rejected?

Unfortunately, sometimes lawyers must turn down cases. In order for a lawyer to accept a case, he or she must consider many factors, including the severity of your injuries, which parties were at fault, conflicts of interests, legal limitations, time constraints and more. If the firm decides that it cannot handle this case for you, that may not necessarily mean that you do not have a case — just that this firm is not in a position to accept your case.

At our firm, turning down cases is one of our least favorite parts of our work. When we have to tell clients that we cannot take their cases, we do our best to refer them to a local bar association or another lawyer who is better suited to help. We also try to provide them with educational materials, like this book, to help them better understand the system and where their cases may fit into it.

CHAPTER FOUR

YOU HAVE BECOME A PLAINTIFF — WHAT NOW?

You have been injured through someone else's actions, and you know you may be entitled to recover financial damages. You have decided to hire a lawyer to represent you and bring a legal claim for these damages. You are now a plaintiff.

The most important thing for you to do now is focus on getting better. That means you need to follow your doctor's advice and keep all of your appointments. If your doctor prescribes physical therapy, tests or other medical procedures, you should follow through with his or her recommendation. If your doctor writes you a prescription for medication to help you heal or manage your pain, you should not delay having it filled at the pharmacy.

Not only will this help you heal, but it also creates a "paper trail" that will be important for your personal injury lawsuit. Your doctors' records often act as the medical testimony in your case and help the lawyer determine the value of your claim. It is vital to be careful about following through with your doctors' recommendations.

Keeping Diaries and Calendars

Your lawyer may ask you to keep a diary, a calendar of your daily activities or both, focusing on your physical and psychological injuries. This may seem like a chore, but it can be important for your legal case because it helps to prove your claims about your injuries, your pain and how they affect your life. If you sustained serious injuries in the accident, your treatment may continue for months and your healing patterns may change over time. It is important to keep a record of the changes you notice, both positive and negative, starting as soon as possible after the accident.

In some cases, even your treating physician may benefit from your notes.

YOUR DIARY MATTERS

Clients and potential clients frequently tell personal injury lawyers "I am not the suing type." Many people are injured by someone else's wrongful or negligent act, yet they are either afraid of litigating or do not know what it takes to bring a claim. Essentially, bringing a claim means that you become a plaintiff, and this may seem like a daunting task to many people. However, the simplest tasks assigned to plaintiffs can often have huge rewards.

This was the case for one client who came looking for lawyer nearly two years after his accident. He was severely injured when his van was run off the road by an unknown driver, causing his right arm to be paralyzed. He told his lawyer that he waited so long to get legal help because he assumed there was no one to collect from, since the car that caused the accident was never located. He did, however, keep a diary of his daily life over the two years since his accident. In it, he noted every time a nurse came to his house, every time his mother had to drive him to therapy and even how excruciating the pain was on a daily basis.

After investigating, his lawyer discovered that the client's company van had uninsured motorist insurance that should cover the accident. After a two-week trial, he was awarded a multimillion dollar verdict. This diary of his life was very important because it helped explain to the jury all that he had been through. Even though he did not know at the time that he would eventually become a plaintiff, common sense dictated much of what he did that resulted in such a large recovery.

In your diary, you should focus on how you feel and how you are coping with your injuries. Make these entries as often as you feel a change; there is no need to make an entry every day. To begin, write down your name and a start date. On any day after the accident when you notice any changes in how you feel, or experience anything unusual, write it down. Include the date and a brief description of what you are feeling and what you were doing when you felt it. Include any descriptions of things that seem important, such as events that seem to trigger pain.

It is important not to forget the diary as time goes on. At the beginning, you may make daily entries, but as you start to feel better, you may find yourself making entries that are further and further apart. It is absolutely fine to make fewer entries if you have less to say, but it is important not to forget your diary altogether. Unfortunately, some injuries continue to have occasional side effects, even after they seem to have healed. Try not to tuck your diary so far out of sight that you forget about it.

You should use the calendar to record each of your doctor's appointments or other medical care. When you record a diagnostic appointment, be sure to note the type of test, such as an MRI. It is better not use this calendar to record social appointments or chores that are not relevant to your case. However, you should also record the dates and times of appointments with your lawyer, and any deadlines or court dates he or she provides.

You should take your diary and calendar with you both to doctor's appointments and to meetings with your lawyer. They will help your doctor treat you better and keep your lawyer updated on your injuries and how they are healing.

Pre-Litigation Settlement

Many of our clients are surprised to learn that they might be able to settle their cases before they even file their lawsuits. In fact, a significant percentage of personal injury cases are settled during the beginning stages of the case. This is possible because part of the job of a personal injury lawyer is to negotiate with insurance companies, both your own and the company or companies for the other parties involved. This type of quick settlement is most likely when there is little or no question that the other driver is liable for your injuries, such as when the driver has admitted responsibility, or when he or she got a ticket. It may also happen when liability is still in question, but your injuries are especially severe.

FOLLOW YOUR DOCTOR'S ORDERS

Following your doctor's recommendations will help you recover as well as possible, but it will also help your case. That was underscored by one trial involving a woman who was rear-ended by another driver while she was parked behind a stopped school bus.

After the crash, which was obviously the defendant's fault, the plaintiff was taken to the hospital with complaints of back and neck pain. After taking X-rays and examining the plaintiff, the emergency room doctor instructed the plaintiff to "follow up with your medical doctor if you continue to have problems."

The next day, the plaintiff still had back pain. She called her chiropractor and received treatment for her crash-related injuries. At trial, the defendant argued that the plaintiff did not follow her doctor's orders because she saw a chiropractor rather than a medical doctor.

The jury returned a five-figure verdict for the plaintiff but reduced the award by several thousand dollars because she saw a chiropractor rather than a medical doctor. Fortunately, the judge corrected the jury's decision and awarded the plaintiff the full original amount. (Judges may not do this in every state.) However, if the judge had not done this, the woman's failure to follow the exact recommendation of her doctor would have resulted in a verdict that penalized her for it.

During the pre-litigation process, your lawyer verifies that the liable person or people have insurance coverage, and determines whether your own insurance policy provides coverage for the accident. Your lawyer will also investigate the facts surrounding the accident, reviewing the police report, interviewing the witnesses and inspecting the scene of the accident in order to get the best possible information on how the accident occurred and who is at fault. And he or she will also review your current and prior medical records, to prove that your injuries stem from the accident and understand how they relate to any preexisting medical condition.

Once your lawyer has done all of this, he or she can begin to determine what your legal claim may be worth, financially. This is generally expressed as a range of values (such as $200,000 to $500,000), because of the uncertainty of settlement negotiations and trials. But rest assured that your lawyer will never settle your claim for less than it is truly worth.

At some point during the course of your medical treatment, your lawyer will demand a settlement from the insurance company, in an effort to get the compensation you are entitled to without a formal lawsuit. Usually, the insurance company will respond with either an offer to settle or a request for additional information. That additional information may include copies of MRI films, tax returns, records of a physical examination of you by a doctor of your choosing or other information the insurance company feels is important in understanding your case. Once it has all of the necessary information, it will be in a position to make a settlement offer. Your lawyer will notify you of this offer so that you can discuss it and determine whether you find the offer acceptable.

Pre-Litigation Mediation

Sometimes, but not often, the parties will agree to mediation before continuing to litigation. The mediation may come at the suggestion of either the insurance adjuster or your own lawyer. Mediation allows both sides to present the relevant facts of the case and the extent of the costs and damages to an independent third party, a mediator, who will work to help them agree on a settlement. These independent mediators are often retired judges or people with special court certification as mediators, so they should have experience with the laws and issues that are important in your case. (For more on mediation and other forms of alternative dispute resolution, see Chapter Six.)

If no settlement is reached at mediation, the case is free to proceed to litigation. Any failure to settle at mediation will have no effect on your right to continue your case.

The Case Settles

If a settlement is reached, either through negotiation or pre-litigation mediation, the insurance company will send a check for you. They will also send a legal document called a release for you (and if necessary, your spouse) to sign. By signing the release, you relieve the insurance company and the party who is liable for your injuries of any further obligations or payments related to the injuries and damages from the accident. You must sign this release in order to collect the settlement.

Your lawyer should have a trust account, which holds money that has been entrusted to him or her but belongs to clients. Once the settlement funds clear through this trust account, your lawyer will prepare a settlement statement or closing statement for your signature. This is another legal document, which sets forth the total amount of the settlement and any deductions for lawyers' fees and costs, or any medical bills or liens that should be paid from the settlement. You will have the opportunity to review this statement, and your signature will authorize the law firm to send you your settlement funds. Once you receive the proceeds from the settlement, your case is successfully concluded. For more on settling and closing your case, please see Chapter Six.

CHAPTER FIVE

LITIGATION

Even though many claims are resolved before a lawsuit is formally filed, there are some insurers that simply refuse to settle a claim for a fair amount. The extent of your injuries, the type of accident you had, the amount of insurance coverage available, who was at fault and the difficulty of proving that fault are all factors that could prevent you from reaching a fair and quick settlement with the insurance company. If you are unable reach a fair settlement, your lawyer will probably recommend filing a lawsuit. However, even if a lawsuit is filed, your lawyer will almost certainly continue trying to settle your case before the trial.

When Do You File Your Lawsuit?

The law of each state sets deadlines by which you must file your lawsuit. These are called statutes of limitations, and they are usually calculated either from the date of your injury or from the date you discovered an injury that was not immediately obvious. (They may also be extended for minors and people with certain disabilities.) For example, the statute of limitations for personal injury lawsuits stemming from motor vehicle accidents in Colorado is three years. Statutes of limitations are different in each state and often change according to the type of case you have, but all of them are hard deadlines. That is, if you wait too long, you will not be able to pursue your case, no matter how strong it is. One of the first things your lawyer will do after learning about your case is calculate the statute of limitations that applies, and take any action necessary to preserve your right to sue.

There are also legal deadlines that apply in certain specific circumstances. For example, if you plan to sue a government agency, you are frequently required to give that agency notice within a relatively short period of time, or file an administrative complaint, before you may sue.

YOUR RECORDS ARE ESSENTIAL IN DISCOVERY

As a plaintiff, you now have the responsibility to prove your case. But ironically, the defendant does not have to prove anything. Because the burden to prove your case is on you, your actions as a plaintiff are very important. Take the case of a 37-year-old construction worker who was hurt when a load of cement blocks was partially dropped on him, driving him to his knees. This injury caused him debilitating back pain, and because of it, he was never able to return to work.

The problem in the case was that all of the damages were based on an invisible injury — pain. Pain is very difficult to prove. But in this case, the injured worker was extremely consistent about attending all of his medical appointments, kept very good records, established reliability with his medical providers and had a long-established reputation for honesty and hard work.

Because of this consistency and reliability, all of the witnesses in the case were willing and able to give favorable testimony. The injured man's medical providers were able to explain and support his claim for the unseen injuries. As a result, his lawyers were able to convince the defendants of the substantial risk of taking the case to trial, winning an out-of-court settlement large enough to supplement the man's lost income and provide security for his family. In his role as a plaintiff, the worker did his job successfully so that his lawyers could do theirs.

Because these deadlines can be as short as 30 days, and because missing them can take away your right to sue, it is essential to learn about them and take action as quickly as possible. This is one reason why personal injury lawyers prefer to see you as soon as is practical after your accident.

Filing a Lawsuit

Your lawyer's office should take care of the actual, formal filing of the lawsuit. But in general, you will file your case in the county where your accident happened, or in the county where one or both of the parties involved lives, depending on the circumstances and the laws of your state. The county where the case is filed is sometimes called the "venue." Your lawyer can explain how these rules affect your case.

A lawsuit formally starts when you file a written complaint or petition with the court. This complaint first describes the facts of the case, your injuries and why the person you are suing is responsible for your injuries. It then separately lists each "cause of action," which is a reason for suing, and finishes with a request for financial compensation for the injuries you have listed. This can be quite detailed, depending on your state's requirements, but it always contains enough information to tell the plaintiffs why they are being sued.

Along with the complaint, your lawyer will also file a summons or citation, a document that will be served to (that is, formally given to) the defendants. The summons explains how the defendants should respond to the complaint and gives the deadline to do so. As a courtesy, your lawyer may send a copy of the complaint to the defendants' insurance company or companies.

When this complaint is filed, your lawyer will also specify whether you prefer a trial by jury or a "bench trial," in which a judge makes most of the decisions. You and your lawyer should have agreed on this ahead of time. In a jury trial, a group of randomly selected citizens from the area decides all of the questions of fact while the judge acts as a referee and resolves legal questions. By contrast, in a bench trial, a judge decides questions of fact as well as questions about the law. Bench trials are less common than jury trials. If your lawyer recommends one, he or she should be able to explain why.

Who Answers the Complaint?

After the complaint is filed and served, the defendant's insurance company will usually assign the matter internally to an employee called a litigation claims adjuster, who will oversee the claim. This person's job is to try to resolve your claim before trial, or handle the claim in a way that helps the insurer at trial. Insurance companies do not like to be sued, of course; they may take extra steps to resolve your claim after the lawsuit is filed, so you may be able to settle at this stage. However, for this chapter, we will assume that you will not settle right away.

The insurance company will also assign one of its own lawyers, or hire an outside lawyer, to represent the defendant in court. The first task for this lawyer is to prepare a document called an answer to file with the court. This answer will either admit or deny the allegations of your complaint; it may even say that other parties are at fault for your injuries and should be added to the lawsuit. The answer may also set forth any defenses the defendant is planning to use in the case that explain why he or she is not responsible for your injuries.

It is only after the answer is filed that a trial in your case will be scheduled. If the defendant fails to file an answer at all or breaks a rule when filing it, you can ask the court to simply declare you the winner by asking for a "default judgment." This is not common; it is a little like a sports team forfeiting a game because it never showed up to the playing field.

Discovery

Discovery is the process of exchanging information about the case with the other side of a lawsuit. This is a formal legal process governed by set rules. The law requires that both sides of a lawsuit share information about the case with one another on request. (Certain things, such as privileged communications between you and your lawyer, are exempt from discovery even if they are specifically requested.) In most cases, the information exchanged includes information about your accident, the injuries you sustained, the nature and cost of your health care, the effect of your injuries on your life and your family, your employment background and your educational background.

Discovery is extremely important because it permits both parties to learn about the facts and issues of the lawsuit before trial. This allows both sides to build a case and evaluate the strengths and weaknesses of their positions. During settlement talks, the information you receive during discovery can be invaluable.

THE IMPORTANCE OF BEING EARNEST DURING DISCOVERY

Complete disclosure of information during discovery is an important way to come to a settlement, but it is also important if you end up in trial. This was illustrated by the case of a client who failed to inform her lawyer that she had been denied a promotion at work because of her injuries, resulting in over $20,000 a year in lost income. She thought it would be better to "surprise" the insurance company with this information at trial.

However, because this client had failed to bring this information up in discovery, the defendant was able to prevent her from testifying about it at trial because they had not had an opportunity to investigate that part of her claim. The judge ruled that because the information was not provided before trial, as required by the rules of discovery, it could not be presented to the jury.

This mistake by the client prevented her from recovering compensation for lost wages that totaled $400,000 over her lifetime. The client still won her lawsuit, but the judgment did not include any compensation for her lost future income. Not only could she have won more by disclosing this loss before trial, but she could also have increased her chances of settling the claim for a larger amount — without going to trial at all.

Interrogatories

Typically, the first step for both sides in discovery is to send written questions for the other side to answer. These written questions are called interrogatories, and in many areas, you will answer these questions under oath, even though they are written and you will not be in a courtroom. Interrogatories will usually ask you about the accident, your background and your damages, including any past injuries or problems for which you have sought health care, as well as any previous legal claims you were involved with. You may also be asked to provide details about any income you lost or information about your past employment. The goal is to build a story about the relevant parts of your life before and after the accident. When you have written your answers, you will sign them and they will be sent to the defendant's lawyer.

We find that some clients are initially reluctant to answer these questions, because they can be personal or stray into topics considered impolite or irrelevant. Your lawyer can and will formally object to an inappropriate interrogatory, or to a number of interrogatories that exceeds limits set by your state's laws. However, these questions are usually being asked because they are relevant to your case. Most of the information about your health and your finances is considered "discoverable," which means it is a fair question during discovery. Your responses help your own lawyer and the other side gather the information they need to evaluate your claim, which helps you get closer to settling your case fairly.

Requests for Admissions

Another written discovery tool is a request for admissions, which is simply a document asking one side to admit or deny the facts it specifies. When you might get these requests depends on the rules of your court. If you dispute or deny a request for admissions, you must write down the facts that you believe support your position. Your lawyer should help you with this. Using requests for admissions helps both sides determine which facts are agreed upon, which are disputed and which must be part of the lawsuit.

It is important to respond to requests for admissions in a timely manner, because if you miss the specified deadline, the court will behave as if you admitted to everything asserted in the request.

Requests for Production

Requests for production of documents — that is, asking the other side to send copies of specific papers — are an important part of discovery. Requests for production may come with the interrogatories, but both sides are free to request production of documents throughout discovery.

Requests for production should be requests for documents that are relevant to the lawsuit, the accident or your damages. This often includes copies of your health care records, receipts or invoices for your health care expenses, accident reports, witness statements and pictures of the scene of the accident. If you are claiming a loss of income, you will probably be asked to provide your tax returns for several years prior to the accident. You may even be asked to produce any notes or diaries you have kept. But either side may request any discoverable document. Your lawyer may review the request for production with you and help you copy the documents and send them to the defendant's lawyer.

In addition to requesting documents and evidence from you, the defendant's lawyer may also ask other people or companies for information. Most commonly, he or she may request copies of your medical records directly from your treating doctors. The defendant may also be entitled to request information about you from your employers, schools you have attended or from the military, if you have served. Additionally, if you have applied for Social Security benefits, the defendant's lawyer may request information about your claim from the Social Security Administration. You may feel uncomfortable with these requests, but if the information is discoverable, the defendant's lawyer is entitled to ask for these documents. In fact, you may even be required to sign forms authorizing release of the information.

Depositions

A deposition is a little like an oral version of interrogatories. When you give a deposition, you answer questions from the lawyer for the defendant in person, under oath, and usually with all of the parties and their lawyers in the room. A court reporter will be hired to take down your answers, which you usually give in the office of the court reporter or one of the lawyers. Either side may request a deposition at any time, but the request is most likely to come after you have responded to interrogatories and requests for production of documents.

Many of our clients are nervous before depositions, but there is no need to be nervous. Your lawyer will be there to observe throughout the deposition and can object to inappropriate questions or ask for breaks if you need them. This is important, because it is essential for you to stay calm and professional during a deposition. This is the first opportunity for the other side to evaluate you in person, so you should appear neat and as confident as possible. Your lawyer can advise you on what to wear and how to behave.

Your lawyer (or his or her staff) should prepare you ahead of time for the questions in your deposition. You may be asked to attend a meeting where you review all of the written information your lawyer has, as well as any responses you gave to interrogatories. It is especially important to make sure that your testimony is truthful and consistent with these interrogatory responses, because the lawyer for the defendant will probably question you closely about any inconsistencies. This process should also help refresh your memory about the details of your injuries, your treatment and your recovery.

When the deposition begins, you will be asked to swear an oath to tell the truth to the best of your knowledge, just as you would in court. The court reporter will swear you in, then type your testimony into a written transcript that will be available to the lawyers later. In some cases, the deposition is also videotaped, which means that there will be another person operating a video camera and filming the deposition. The lawyer taking your deposition will introduce him- or herself and may briefly explain the procedure for the deposition.

At your deposition, you will probably start by reviewing the information in your written interrogatory responses. The deposition is an opportunity for the other side's lawyer to clarify or have you explain those written answers, and to obtain additional information. As we said, it is important to make sure that your testimony is truthful and consistent with your interrogatory responses, so the other lawyer does not spy a seeming inconsistency between your oral testimony and your written testimony. Your answers should be based on your own personal knowledge; do not guess in making an answer. If you do not know or remember the answer to a question, you should say so. Many people feel embarrassed to admit they do not know something or had a memory lapse, but these things are only human. And when you are under oath, it is important to be as straightforward as possible.

Remember that the lawyer for the insurance company is your adversary, not your friend, and may not believe the facts are the way you say they are. If you are asked a question that you disagree with, perhaps because it assumes something you do not believe is true, do not be afraid to say so in order to answer the question. Stay in control; if the lawyer for the defendant puts you in a position where you must speculate, say so. If you do not understand or hear a question, you can ask for it to be repeated or rephrased.

As with the written discovery, you may feel that some of the questions are invasive or do not directly relate to your accident. However, unless your lawyer objects or tells you not to respond, you should answer every question in the most honest way you can. If some of the questions upset you, you can usually take a break during your deposition testimony, although you may have to respond to any unanswered questions first. If you would like a break, you can simply tell your lawyer. If the break is allowed, you will be permitted to get up, walk around, get a drink of water or just clear your head.

After the other side has finished questioning you, your lawyer is usually permitted to ask you more questions, or clarify an answer you gave earlier. This does not happen in every case, and in many instances, your lawyer may not ask you any questions at all. If this is the case, it does not mean the lawyer failed to do his or her job;

there may be strategic reasons.

In addition to taking your deposition, the lawyers in the case may also depose (take a deposition from) any other witness in the case. While the number of depositions will vary from case to case, depositions are often taken from the defendant, any witnesses to the accident, friends and family members who are familiar with your injuries, representatives from the defendant's insurance company and your own doctors and health care providers.

Discovery and Settlement

The discovery tools outlined in this chapter are only some of those available in a lawsuit, but these will be used in the majority of cases. Discovery may seem time-consuming, but by exchanging this information, the parties can often get the information they need to settle the case without a trial. And if the parties are still not able to resolve their case after discovery, the information they exchange during discovery will help them build evidence for their cases and narrow down which facts must be decided at trial.

CHAPTER SIX

SETTLEMENT

Many cases settle voluntarily, without having to go to trial. Trials take time, are expensive and may make clients nervous. They can also produce unexpected outcomes. From a personal perspective, an experienced personal injury lawyer may want to take a case to trial — but that is always the client's decision. The job of an experienced personal injury lawyer is to help clients achieve their goals. We find that most of the time, the client wants the matter resolved quickly and fairly, so settlement is always in mind. If no settlement offer meets the client's goals, the matter can be resolved by trial.

Experienced personal injury lawyers also understand that settlement should not be rushed. Settling a case is a *process.* It is a dialogue and can be complex. Different lawyers initiate the process in different ways (who goes first and so forth), but it always ends up with an offer and a series of counteroffers and counter-demands. This is the process, and there is more to it than simply passing numbers back and forth. Behind the numbers is reasoning. It is through this dialogue that the case is, hopefully, resolved. Each side has an opportunity to persuade the other. By exploring the weaknesses and strengths of each side's case, the parties will generally be able to either agree on settlement or agree that they need the help of a judge or a jury. Either way, they make forward progress — and reasonable decisions.

Be wary of settlement offers that come very early in this process, even if it is tempting to end the case quickly. After many years of practice, we have found that insurance companies will often offer a settlement before clients and their lawyers can determine all of their damages. Or a settlement offer will be extended quickly by an insurance company, before all the liens and other expenses have been determined. Everyone wants the matter resolved as quickly as possible — but an experienced personal injury lawyer knows that a fast settlement offer by an insurance company can be a trap.

Deciding whether to accept a settlement offer requires you to consider subjective as well as objective factors. For example, there are benefits to ending your claim, and it may also be a personal relief. On the other hand, the time, anxiety, energy and risk assumption required to go to trial may be worth it for the client —because of the potential for greater compensation, for an important lesson to be learned or for an important message to be sent. The decision does not always turn on the money alone. Client objectives vary, and each case and each client is different. The settlement process offers an opportunity for dialogue — and out of this dialogue comes a decision that fits the client in *that* case.

There are numerous factors to think about when considering a settlement offer, but issues to consider start with the amount of money being offered, the conditions attached to the offer and the amounts owed to third parties — like health care providers or other insurance companies. There are laws and contractual obligations that govern these third parties' rights to participate in the distribution of settlement proceeds. These rules are part of every settlement agreement, and you are expected to know them. An insurance company has no duty to explain the rules to you. Third parties such as health care providers might also claim part of your settlement behind the scenes.

What you and your law firm must determine is the true *value* of the offer being extended. That is, you need to know how much of the money offered will end up in your pocket. To answer this question, the lawyer has to solve the puzzle (so to speak) that is the totality of the client's claim, with the goal of maximizing the claim's value. An experienced personal injury lawyer will analyze these and other issues behind the scenes, so the client can focus on the challenge of recovering from injuries and putting his or her life back together.

The lawyer participates in settling cases — but it is always the client who makes the final decision. The lawyer's job is to prepare the client to make that decision fully informed. And, of course, the lawyer will provide the benefit of his or her education and experience, as well as perspective that can be valuable for clients who may be upset and angry about their injuries. Emotions play a part in decisions on settlements, of course, but they should not be the only criteria. Your lawyer will help you strike a proper balance as you go through the process.

Sometimes the courtroom is the right choice, if the client makes that decision with the advice of an experienced personal injury lawyer. Understand, however, that your lawyer will work to give you a realistic assessment of the benefits and risks associated with settlement and trial. That way, you can make an informed choice.

Understanding a Settlement Offer

In a settlement, there is always paperwork. Before you agree to a settlement offer, you and your lawyer will discuss whether you understand and accept all of the terms and conditions of the settlement. The insurance company for the at-fault party will ask you to accept money in exchange for your agreement to end the case — releasing the at-fault party from any future responsibility.

First and foremost, you and your lawyer will discuss whether the amount of the offer is reasonable under the circumstances. Your lawyer should be able to give you a professional opinion on this, weighing the likely outcome of a trial against the certainty and benefits of settling now. Rejecting one settlement offer does not mean you will never get another. In fact, some defendants even expect to go through several rounds of offers and rejections.

Another consideration is any debt, claim or lien that you might owe to health care providers or other parties because of the accident. (We will discuss and define liens in the next section.) If the settlement offer is not be sufficient to pay all of these debts, you may be liable for the rest. Sometimes, your lawyer can help by negotiating or using other remedies available under the law to make sure all of your obligations are covered. Depending on the circumstances, your lawyer might be able to convince creditors to take a lesser amount in exchange for immediate payment. But because this is an uncertain process, it is important to discuss your debts and obligations with your lawyer when analyzing a settlement offer.

QUICK RESULTS HELP FAMILY IN NEED

Sometimes, a quick settlement is one of the most important services a personal injury lawyer can provide, as with one tragic wrongful death case. In this case, a young and growing family was in a serious car accident that killed the wife and her unborn child, leaving the husband a single parent of a 2-year-old. Thankfully, the 2-year-old was not seriously injured. The husband, his mother and his child filed a wrongful death and personal injury lawsuit.

Because the driver responsible for the accident did not have substantial assets, the family's law firm knew it was important to identify and collect from all available insurance policies. The firm worked quickly and was able settle these claims in just eight months, for an amount exceeding $1 million. Although that money could never bring back their lost loved ones, receiving this large so quickly allowed this grieving father and husband to move on with his life and take care of his child.

At this stage, your lawyer may also talk to you about subrogation, which we discussed a little in Chapter One. A subrogation claim is a claim that an insurance company or other party has on the money you recover in your case. For example, if you have medical insurance, it probably covered your initial medical care. But if an auto insurance company is legally obligated to cover those costs, the medical insurer may be entitled to reimbursement from the auto insurer or from you, out of any settlement you reach with the auto insurer. Subrogation can be complex and depends on state and federal laws as well as individual contracts. Your lawyer should help you understand how it applies to you.

If you have claims against more than one defendant or insurance company, or are considering a lawsuit over the same injuries against another party, you should also consider whether settling with one defendant could limit or eliminate your right to pursue the other cases. For example, in states with at-fault auto insurance, you may have a claim against your own auto insurer for unpaid uninsured/underinsured auto insurance claims. (Much more about insurance can be found in Chapter One.) Many states require you to notify other parties if you settle with one. If you fail to follow this or other laws, you may lose your right to pursue your other claims.

How Liens Could Affect Your Settlement

Liens are legal claims against personal property, used to secure a debt. A residential mortgage is a common type of lien. A lien claim might be a part of your case if you have a large amount of debt stemming from the accident and you cannot pay it out of your own pocket. This is particularly common with debts for medical care. If this is the case, the hospital or other medical provider that you owe money to can eventually put a lien on your settlement, or on your home or other property. Liens make it difficult to sell or otherwise make changes to the property.

Resolving lien claims can be difficult because of the many complex laws that apply to them, and because holders of lien claims are often slow to respond in writing to questions about their liens. Unfortunately, the law does not always say that lienholders are required to respond to requests for a lien amount within a specific time, and it sometimes takes months to get an appropriate answer. This delay prevents prompt payments of settlement funds to clients like you, and can be frustrating for you and your lawyer. Your law firm should work hard to obtain this information and resolve these issues, so that the settlement can be distributed and you can resolve your case.

For example, if Medicaid or Medicare has paid health care providers for treatment you needed because of your accident, they are entitled to reimbursement of those payments. To ensure that they are paid, they may place a lien on your settlement. Your lawyer will probably have to hold back a part of your settlement equal to the debt until you can negotiate an agreement and pay the agency.

TAKE CARE WITH MEDICARE

Cases involving Medicare can be much more complicated than cases involving private insurers. One family using Medicare found that out after the mother was seriously hurt in a car accident. They were unable to resolve their claim with the wrongdoer's insurance company, so they hired an experienced personal injury lawyer. After the lawyer was able to settle the case for $100,000, the family thought that their life would turn around. However, they soon discovered that Medicare was demanding all of the settlement proceeds for reimbursement of the medical bills it had paid on the mother's behalf. In fact, Medicare claimed it should be reimbursed for all medical care provided to the mother for the last five years, even though the accident had only happened a year earlier.

Their experienced personal injury lawyer was able to distinguish the charges for treatment of the auto accident injuries from the other types of treatment. Medicare, because it is a government entity without any true controls, took months to consider the case. After extensive negotiations with Medicare, the lawyer was able to substantially reduce Medicare's claim, to an amount allowing this needy family to retain enough money to help pay the mother's future medical expenses and replace their car.

When multiple insurers or debts are involved, this can become quite complex. For example, you might run into complicated lien problems when you have your own private insurance (including a settlement from a personal injury case) but are using Medicare as a secondary insurer. When it is not certain whether Medicare is a primary or secondary insurer, Medicare will make a conditional payment. If it is later determined that some other party was responsible for that payment, Medicare is entitled to a refund from that party, or from you or the health care provider, if one of you was paid by that party. The federal government may place a lien on your property to recover this type of conditional payment. (It might also be entitled to make a subrogation claim against your settlement.) Again, your settlement funds cannot be distributed until you reach an agreement and pay Medicare.

Ways to Reach a Settlement

In this book, we have referred a few times to "settlement negotiations." However, negotiating directly with the defendant and his or her lawyer is just one way you can reach a settlement. You can also use methods that are collectively called "alternative dispute resolution," which are more formal. They include mediation and arbitration, both of which are a little like informal trials led by someone specifically trained in resolving disputes. In some states, courts may order the parties to try an alternative dispute resolution method, or you may be obligated by a contract to try it. You can also choose this on your own.

Direct Negotiations

The most direct way to reach a settlement is simply to negotiate with the insurance adjuster, or the defendant and the defendant's lawyer. Doing this requires substantial knowledge in two areas: The prospects of your case if you go to trial and the value of your claim. This is where having a lawyer can benefit you greatly. Experienced personal injury lawyers have handled hundreds or even thousands of cases like yours, so they understand how your case is likely to come out at trial. They should also be familiar with the courts and juries in your area. For the same reasons, they understand how to calculate the full value of your claim. And of course, a lawyer is an experienced negotiator. This levels the playing field against the insurance adjuster or defense lawyer, who will work to minimize your payments to save money for the insurance company.

Once you retain a law firm, it will handle all contact and

negotiations with the insurance company and the defendant. Legally, they can no longer contact you directly, so the law firm will take care of it for you. Under most circumstances, you do not need to be present for direct settlement negotiations, although your lawyer will keep you informed throughout. Using the information you provided about your case and the information obtained during discovery, your lawyer will build the strongest possible case for settlement and present it to the other side. If they make an offer, your lawyer will present it to you for a decision, along with his or her advice. As we said before, this is 100 percent your decision.

Mediation

Mediation is a type of settlement negotiation in which an impartial third party helps both sides come to an agreement, using training in dispute resolution methods and legal experience. Mediation is usually conducted through an in-person discussion with all parties, including you, the insurance company and/or the defendant, as well as the lawyers for all parties. Generally speaking, a mediator is a retired judge, a lawyer or other neutral person who has also been trained to mediate disputes. Frequently, he or she has a special certification from the courts or the bar association of your state. However, unlike a judge, a mediator must be paid. Usually, you and the defendant will split this cost evenly. Mediation can be chosen or ordered by the court at any time during your case, although it is more likely after discovery has been conducted.

At a mediation conference, both sides will sit down and present their cases to the mediator informally. There is no jury. The mediator will then discuss each party's claims, either in the same room or in private conferences, if necessary. In these conferences, the mediator might ask questions and raise issues to help the parties find a compromise that they can agree to. Because the mediator is experienced in the law affecting your case, he or she should take into account your legal rights, the extent of your injuries and the prospects of your case in a trial.

After the initial mediation conference, you may have a follow-up conference or discuss the matter by telephone. It is important to realize that coming to an agreement in this way can be slow. If you reach an agreement at mediation, it is not binding unless you and the defendant sign papers and take other steps to formalize it. If you do not come to an agreement, you are free to try again or continue toward trial.

In mediation, you are in a way previewing your case for the other side, just as they are previewing theirs for you. That means it is important to be careful about what you say and to present yourself in a professional manner, just as you would if you were going to trial. A good rule of thumb is to behave as if the room is full of a diverse group of people from your area, some of whom may not be sympathetic to you. Your lawyer will prepare you for mediation, just as he or she would for trial and depositions. And if you cannot attend a mediation conference, you should let your lawyer know as soon as you can, because not showing up might result in penalties or even the dismissal of your case.

Arbitration

Arbitration is another form of alternative dispute resolution. Like mediation, it brings the parties together before an impartial third party who understands the applicable law and will keep order during discussions. And like mediators, arbitrators are often retired judges or lawyers with experience in the legal area affecting your case, with a fee that will usually be split evenly between the parties. But unlike a mediator, an arbitrator does not actively guide the conversation or give opinions. Arbitrators are more like judges who keep order and rule on questions about the law, and eventually, on which party should prevail. In non-binding arbitration, the resulting judgment is only a suggestion; in binding arbitration, the decision is usually final.

At a non-binding arbitration, both parties present their cases as they would in mediation. But instead of holding the conference that a mediator would hold, an arbitrator simply decides which side should prevail and how much the plaintiff might be entitled to in damages. The idea is to show the parties how an impartial person sees their case, which encourages them to settle. The arbitrator's decision is non-binding, so if you do not agree, you are free to continue to trial. However, in some jurisdictions, you may be penalized for this if the court ordered the arbitration, or if you go to trial and do not do as well. Your lawyer should be able to tell you about the rules that apply to your case.

Binding arbitration is just like non-binding arbitration, except that both parties agree beforehand to abide by the arbitrator's judgment. You and your lawyer can choose binding arbitration, or you may be contractually obligated to use it. Binding arbitration can be advantageous for parties who want to resolve their cases more quickly, and sometimes more cheaply, than they might be able to in court. However, because it is hard to challenge the judgment produced by binding arbitration, it is important to understand before the arbitration that you usually must follow the decision of the arbitrator. In fact, you may be penalized for ignoring or defying that decision. Your lawyer can give you a professional opinion on whether binding arbitration is a good idea in your case.

Closing Your Case

Reaching a settlement can provide some satisfaction in knowing that your legal claim is finally going to be behind you. But you must still complete the closing process, which is an important part of finalizing your case and can take time.

Usually, you will be asked to sign a form called a release that formally concludes all current and future claims against the at-fault party and/or insurance company for these injuries. Because signing this ends your right to collect any more compensation for your injuries from this defendant, you should understand this completely and raise any objections before you sign it. Do not hesitate to bring up questions or concerns with your lawyer. After it is signed, both sides will notify the court that the case has been resolved and ask to dismiss any lawsuit.

As part of the closing process, your lawyer may have to address outstanding bills, claims or liens on your settlement proceeds, as discussed in the section entitled "Understanding a Settlement Offer." This may mean that you have to pay some of your settlement to a third party, or that part of your settlement payment may be held by your lawyer while questions about payment are resolved.

Settlement proceeds are sent directly to your law firm. Injury law firms have bank accounts called trust accounts, where they hold money belonging to clients until their cases are finalized. (This is a lot like holding money in escrow for people who are buying or selling a home.) Ethics rules forbid lawyers from using this money for their own purposes. Your settlement check will go into this account at first. You will probably sign a statement authorizing the law firm to deposit it.

The net settlement proceeds will be released to you after you sign a form called a closing or settlement statement, which typically ends your case and your client relationship with the law firm. It also lists all of the disbursements of the settlement funds, which includes payment of legal fees and costs, outstanding medical expenses, liens and any other debts to be paid out of the settlement, as well as your own payment. Again, you should not hesitate to bring up any questions or concerns about this document. If you have special circumstances or a particularly complicated case, your lawyer may bring up other ways your settlement proceeds might be disbursed, or have suggestions designed to serve your best financial and legal interests.

Your lawyer cannot write you a settlement check until this paperwork is done. If you are concerned about receiving the money quickly, it is important to take care of the paperwork as soon as possible.

Case Study: Increasing Your Settlement

Hiring an experienced personal injury lawyer may substantially increase your recovery, even if there is limited money available from insurance policies and you have high medical bills. In this section, we would like to show you an example of how a lawyer's negotiations made a difference for one client who was injured in a motorcycle accident. Of course, the facts of each case are unique, so the results may not look much like the results in your case. But we hope we can show you how valuable it can be to get help from an experienced personal injury lawyer when dealing with insurance claims.

The client in this case, a woman in her twenties, was riding on the back of her boyfriend's motorcycle when a tire fell off the back of a tow truck and struck the motorcycle. She was seriously injured in the resulting accident, with medical bills reaching a total of $140,000. The tow truck's insurance company offered her $100,000, which it claimed was the total amount available under the insurance policy covering the tow truck. That is, that was what they claimed *before* she retained a lawyer. Before calling a lawyer, she had worked out an agreement with her medical providers, in which they would receive the entire $100,000 available under the insurance policy, and she would make payments for the remaining amounts due over time.

This victim learned of a lawyer who had many years of experience with accident cases, and called to ask if he had any advice about dealing with outstanding medical bills. The lawyer asked her if she had confirmed that the $100,000 was the only amount available under the tow truck company's insurance policy, or if she had confirmed that this was the only insurance policy that could cover the accident. The lawyer also asked whether any of her medical bills had been paid through a group health insurance policy, if she had reviewed that policy to determine whether one insurer might have to compensate another, and if any agreement was made by the tow truck's insurer with medical providers for paying off the medical bills.

After speaking with the lawyer, the woman realized that there was more to the case, and that she needed help to get the best compensation she could. With help from the lawyer, she was able to reach a settlement with the tow truck company's insurer. Ultimately, the settlement she received in the case paid all of her medical bills and her lawyer's fees, and even provided compensation for her pain, suffering and inconvenience. Most cases are much more complicated than they appear at first. Oftentimes, this is to the benefit of the injured person, as our examples have illustrated.

CHAPTER SEVEN

TRIAL

Once you have been through all of the detailed preparations for a jury trial, you might see why most people prefer not to go to court. People want their disputes solved quickly and fairly. While a trial may be fair, it is rarely quick. Trials require months of preparation, even if the trial itself may take only a few days once you enter the courtroom.

The good news is that many cases handled by experienced personal injury lawyers are settled long before litigation would have started. And in most cases where a lawsuit is filed, the parties still settle before going to the courtroom. It is the collective experience of the lawyers collaborating on this book that 90 percent or more of personal injury cases handled by an experienced personal injury lawyer settle before trial.

This is in part because the job of the personal injury lawyer is to get the fullest possible information to decision-makers on the other side of the case, as early as it can reasonably be shared. Presenting your case before trial lets the defendants know you have a strong case and is aimed at convincing them that settlement may be a better option for both sides. Remember, only you can decide to settle your case. If the other side does not make a fair offer, a jury will be able to decide the dispute.

An experienced personal injury lawyer will prepare your case, from the beginning, just as if it will ultimately go to court. This is not just in case you do go to trial — it is also because full preparation allows you and your lawyer to make the most compelling case possible in settlement talks. The facts will be gathered. The witnesses will be found. The evidence will be assimilated. The issues will be understood. The law will be applied to the facts. Demands for settlement will be presented. Through the settlement discussions, an experienced personal injury lawyer will learn all about the strengths and weaknesses of your claim. If the claim can be settled fairly, so much the better. If not, you will enter your trial ready for litigation.

SOMETIMES, YOU JUST HAVE TO GO TO TRIAL

Sometimes, a trial is necessary in order to reach a fair settlement. That was the case for one 79-year-old man who was badly hurt during an otherwise nice walk at the mall. A kiddie ride had been set up in an open area of the mall, with a ramp leading up to the ride. That ramp was in the walkway and was nearly the same color as the floor. Before the man walked through that area, the owners of a nearby store had reported to the mall security that they had seen numerous shoppers trip and fall over the ramp. Despite this warning, the ride operators took no safety precautions. When the man walked through that area, he tripped and fell. His medical bills exceeded $80,000.

To the man's lawyers, it appeared to be a clear case of negligence — but the defendant denied liability and offered no settlement at all. His law firm filed suit and prepared the case for trial. Still, the defendant offered no money. The law firm took the case to court. After a two-day trial, the jury returned with a verdict of nearly twice the cost of his medical bills.

The Complaint and Answer

Every lawsuit starts with a written complaint filed in court by the lawyer for the plaintiff. The plaintiff's complaint lays out all of the relevant facts, then lists each cause of action (reason for suing), stated as a separate count. At the end of the complaint, the injured party will sum up his or her request for relief in a "prayer." This is a request for damages — financial compensation for your physical, emotional, financial and other injuries. (Please see Chapter Two for more about understanding your injuries.)

The people being sued are called defendants. After your

lawyer files the complaint and has a copy served to the defendants, they must file a written document of their own, called the answer. The answer either admits or denies all of the points raised in the complaint. Because the answer includes reasons for these admissions and denials, it is often your first look at arguments the defendant is likely to make at trial. Together, the complaint and the answer frame the issues the lawsuit will ultimately be about.

Motions

As soon as the case is filed, either side is free to file a motion, which is a request that the court decide a point of law. For example, a defendant may move to dismiss, asking the court to rule that the complaint was filed too late (for example, if the complaint was not filed until after the statute of limitations expired). In considering a defendant's motion to dismiss, the court must assume that allegations in the complaint are true, so that any challenge at this stage is made strictly as a "matter of law" — what the law of your state says about a specific situation. Another example is a motion for summary judgment, which asks the court to rule in the requester's favor because essential facts are no longer in dispute (perhaps because of what has been learned in discovery), making a jury's decision unnecessary.

Either side can also present motions orally, while in the courtroom. Like pre-trial motions, these oral motions ask the court to decide a matter of law. For example, defendants sometimes move for judgment as a matter of law (called a motion for a directed verdict in some states), after the plaintiff has finished presenting evidence. This motion asks the court to dismiss the case without requiring the defendant to present any evidence, asserting that the plaintiff failed to show that a question of material fact is in dispute. Such a motion can address some or all of the many legal issues involved in trying a personal injury claim.

Jury and Bench Trials

When your lawyer files your complaint, he or she will most likely request a jury trial. In a jury trial, a group of randomly selected citizens from your area serve as the "judge of the facts." A jury collectively decides who to believe and what to believe, deciding all questions of disputed fact.

After all evidence is presented, the jury will use directions from the judge (called jury instructions) to decide the three most important questions in any civil trial: fault, causation and damages. Questions of fault ask the jury to decide how much fault each of the parties bears for the injuries. Questions of causation ask the jury to decide whose fault caused what injury. At the end, the jury assigns a dollar value to each injury it believes was caused by the defendants' actions. The jury does all of this according to the judge's instructions and a verdict form provided by the judge.

The judge presiding over a trial, who may also be called the court, is "the judge of the law." His or her job is to preside over all the courtroom proceedings, keeping the trial on track (according to procedural rules) and decide any questions of law. Questions of law can be about either matters of procedure (such as whether a line of questioning is appropriate) or matters of substance (such as whether the defendant may present a certain technical legal defense).

The judge also instructs the jury on how the law affects the facts they are deciding, through the use of jury instructions. For example, if you claim the defendant was negligent, the judge will provide the jury a written a definition of negligence. This definition will be one that has been decided in prior appellate court decisions, or by the state legislature.

There is another type of trial, called a bench trial, in which a judge decides the issues without a jury. If your lawyer thinks you should consider a bench trial, he or she will discuss it with you in advance. As with all aspects of your case, you will make the final decision, using your lawyer's advice.

Burden of Proof

As the party seeking financial damages, the plaintiff has the burden of proof, which means you and your lawyer must provide the evidence to prove that your allegations are true. Many people are familiar with the requirement to prove a case "beyond a reasonable doubt," which is the standard used in a criminal trial. The standard is lower in a personal injury case, because you are seeking a payment, not to put someone in prison. Plaintiffs in personal injury trials must prove their cases "by a preponderance of the evidence," which means the facts you are alleging are more likely than not.

Presenting and Defending the Case

Because you, as the plaintiff, have the burden of proof, your lawyer will present your case first during trial. After your lawyer has presented all of the evidence in support of your complaint, he or she will "rest." Then the defendants will present the evidence in support of their answer.

After each witness testifies for the side that called him or her, the other side has the right to ask questions. This is called cross-examination. A famous legal quotation describes cross-examination as "the greatest legal engine ever invented for the discovery of truth." A good lawyer uses this tool effectively, either to show the strength of the client's case or to show weaknesses in the other side's case. While cross-examination is frequently portrayed by television shows and movies as hostile, it does not have to be hostile in order to be effective.

The Jury Verdict

After all the evidence has been submitted and both sides have rested, the judge will explain the applicable laws to the jury by reading the jury instructions. The jury will then be asked to go to jury room to discuss the evidence in secret. Out of the presence of the judge, the lawyers and the parties, the jury will decide which facts presented are true, apply those facts to the law specified in the jury instructions and attempt to reach an agreement. In order to reach a verdict, the required number of jurors must agree on each point to be decided.

The number of jurors who must agree in order to reach a verdict is different in different jurisdictions. A unanimous verdict is required in federal court, but some state courts allow a verdict even if some of the jurors do not agree with the majority. The rule in your state will be explained by your lawyer. In Colorado, the verdict must be unanimous. If the jury cannot reach a verdict, the court will declare a mistrial, which is sometimes called a "hung jury." When a trial ends with a hung jury, the case has to be retried before a new jury, starting from the beginning.

Judgment and Collection

If the judge believes the jury's verdict was proper, the judge will file a document called the judgment of the court. A verdict in the favor of the injured party is called a plaintiff's judgment. A plaintiff's judgment is a legal document stating that the plaintiff is entitled to collect the payment the jury decided was fair. It shows that the defendant got the due process he or she was entitled to receive and that the defendant is legally being asked to give up property to pay the money awarded by the jury.

If the defendant has an insurance policy that covers this judgment, that insurer will usually pay it without intervention from the court. However, if the defendant or his or her insurance company does not pay voluntarily, you may need to ask the court to force the defendant to comply. This process is called post-judgment collection procedures, and includes requests for documents such as a "writ of execution" or a "writ of garnishment." The purpose of these post-judgment remedies is to seize assets belonging to the defendant so those assets can be sold and the money applied to satisfy the judgment.

If a defendant does not have insurance and does not have assets sufficient to satisfy a judgment, the defendant can file a petition asking that the judgment be discharged. This is done in a bankruptcy court. This is a complicated area of the law and beyond the scope of this book. As a part of the decision to take your personal injury claim through the litigation process, an experienced personal injury lawyer will consider whether a defendant has the ability to pay. This discussion will occur at the beginning of your case. The ability to get paid is always a matter of utmost concern.

The role of an experienced personal injury lawyer is to figure out the end of a case at the beginning, and to work throughout the case to maximize the client's recovery. That work always includes considering whether you will get paid if a verdict is obtained.

Appeals

If either side believes there was a mistake at trial, it can file an appeal. An appeal is a request to another court, called an appeals court, to reconsider the first court's ruling. Most people do not realize that an appeal can only be made on the basis of an error in the law. A jury's decision, as "the judge of the facts," cannot be overturned on appeal unless the jury's decision was somehow the result of an error of law. Appellate courts decide matters of law.

There is no jury in the appeal process. The appellate court judges are required to presume the jury's decisions at trial were correct — as long as the record on appeal contains evidence to support the jury's verdict. A jury's decision can be changed by the appellate court only where there are no facts in the record to support the jury's decision or when the judge who presided over the jury trial allowed the jury to consider facts that should not have been considered, or to incorrectly apply law that was given to the jury. Appellate court decisions are important because they form what is called the common law. The common law is the law of your state, unless a decision of the judicial branch of government is precluded or overturned by a decision of the legislative branch of government.

When the defendant files an appeal, he or she can post a financial bond to stop collection of the judgment. If the appeal fails, that bond will be used to pay the judgment. If you win your case, but the other side appeals, you may have to wait some time before you can collect the compensation you won.

Your lawyer will need to explain this complicated process to you and will counsel you about whether to settle on appeal, given the increased costs, fees and time associated with the complicated appeals process. All of these decisions will turn on the specific facts and law applicable to your case. An experienced personal injury lawyer will explain all of your options and help you make the right decision for you and your family.

It Is the Client's Case

We find that some potential clients are afraid that a lawyer will make important decisions about their cases, such as what settlement amount is fair or whether to file a lawsuit. This is not true. A personal injury claim belongs, at all times, to the client. The lawyer is hired to gather the facts and the law, and to show the client how the law will likely be applied and how the facts will likely be interpreted. As the owner of the claim, the client has the right to make the final decisions about things like whether to settle.

Experienced personal injury lawyers know litigation is a means to an end, not an end in itself. The end is justice for the injured client — full financial compensation for his or her injuries and the satisfaction of holding wrongdoers responsible for their actions. Litigation is simply the means that must be applied when there is a no *voluntary* settlement along the way.

An experienced personal injury lawyer will begin with the end in mind — preparing the claim from the outset in such a way that both the lawyer and the client are ready for litigation and trial — *if necessary.*

CONCLUSION

We wrote this book in order to give you, our clients and potential clients, a helpful and relatively detailed guide to the process of a personal injury claim. We believe this is important information for people who have already decided to pursue a case — but also for those who want more information before they are ready to decide. As a potential client, you have the right to know what you're committing to. And if you become a client, you truly *need* to know these things about your case, for your own peace of mind and to help us make the case as successful as possible.

However, we know that no book can be detailed enough to address every plaintiff's situation. Each case, each pattern of facts and each plaintiff is unique. This is why we want to once again encourage you to meet with us, if you have not already, for more information about what you can expect if you become a plaintiff, tailored to your specific case and your circumstances.

As injury lawyers, we believe that helping people is one of the most important parts of our work. An injury lawsuit helps clients directly by securing money to pay for health care and other costs of an accident, of course, but also by cutting through the bureaucracy of insurers, hospitals and other large organizations to get you the help you need. More indirectly, it can even help the community by alerting others to the dangers that caused your accident, including the at-fault parties' careless or illegal behavior and the lack of oversight or accountability that allowed those behaviors. In a few cases, you may even be able to make new laws or force policy changes that better protect our community.

But no matter what form it takes, a successful resolution to your case is both our goal and our pleasure. There is nothing more fulfilling than being able to make a difference for the better in someone's life. As a plaintiff, you are a partner in that work, and your participation is not just helpful — in many ways, it is essential. We hope that this book has helped you better understand what you can expect from your case, and your own role in making it a success.

ABOUT THE AUTHOR

Attorney Michael R. O'Connell is a personal injury attorney practicing in Colorado with offices in Denver and Breckenridge. His firm, The O'Connell Law Firm, P.C., has successfully handled hundreds of cases for injured people throughout the state. Prior to attending law school, Mr. O'Connell served in the United States Army, and was a research fellow at the National Institutes of Health.

He is a member of Colorado Bar Association, the Colorado Trial Lawyers Association (member, Auto Litigation Committee), American Association for Justice, Denver Bar Association and the National Institute for Trial Advocacy.

Mr. O'Connell is licensed to practice in all jurisdictions in the State of Colorado, as well as in the Federal District Court for Colorado. He frequently lectures physicians and health care practitioners on the finer points of personal injury law, claims and litigation. Mr. O'Connell frequently posts articles and comments on the firm's website at www.coloradoinjuryattorney.net.